SEEING WITH THE EYES OF THE SOUL

VOLUME VI
(2002 - 2007)

REVELATIONS FROM
GOD THE FATHER
TO BARBARA CENTILLI

PITTSBURGH
CENTER for PEACE

To Order additional copies:

Phone: (412) 787-9735
Fax: (412) 787-5204
www.SaintAndrew.com

Contents

Publisher's Foreword

In publishing the revelations contained in this book, I am extremely aware that we are presenting a document of Catholic mysticism that is of the most extraordinary nature. Its contents are not just prophetic, but aim to present the unfolding of a significant, long awaited step in the ongoing fulfillment of salvation history: the restoration of all of God's people, Israel, to their Father and Creator, the Eternal Father of All Mankind.

While perhaps some will retain questions about the interpretation and understanding of the contents of this book, and some will refrain from embracing its revelations until the Church has ruled on their merit, I do want readers to know that the decision to publish this work was arrived at with great care, deliberation and discernment. Our spiritual advisers were strong in their support of its doctrinal soundness and believed that its timely and important revelations were in need of dissemination now. Of course, our obedience to the Catholic Church in this matter is unconditional.

For my own part, I strongly suspect that *Seeing With the Eyes of the Soul* will become a landmark, spiritual classic for generations to come. Its exceptional spirituality, which presents to readers a theological loftiness reflective of the special influence of divine grace, is reminiscent of the texts of the blessed ones throughout Church history.

Indeed, I believe this book will be unforgettable in the minds and hearts of all who read it and will never need a vibrant defense to convince doubters of its authenticity. The words within it speak for themselves with the light of truth and the power of the Holy Spirit.

Most noted is the beautiful "Chaplet Prayers" given by the Father to Barbara. Unlike many private devotions today that emphasize reparation, this prayer appears to be laying the groundwork for future generations to beseech God for the full restoration of His Kingdom (Acts 7:6). Perhaps this chaplet of the Father and its thematic ejaculation, *"I love you Father and I give myself to You",* will become the Rosary of future generations. It is also perhaps reflective of a coming shift in the spiritual consciousness of the Church which may exist after the triumph of God comes into the world.

There are many other revelations in this book just as worthy of contemplation and recognition. But I will refrain from highlighting them, leaving to the reader this pleasant task. Eventually, I believe this book will be embraced by the Church as a great gift from God to His people. Not just a lamp in a time of darkness, but a bright light for mankind to better see and find its way home to its Father–a Father Who hungers to have His Children, and His Kingdom, restored to Him.

Dr. Thomas W. Petrisko
May 13, 1998

OUR FATHER IN HEAVEN

One of the main benefits I personally gained from reading these pages is that they stirred my zeal for souls. I shall return to this theme presently. But first let me say that this account (in the shape of a journal) by Barbara Rose Centilli of her locutions and other religious experiences is in my estimation likely to become a landmark book.

Its author is by no means someone of immature years and unsophisticated background—characteristics common to a number of modern-day mystics. On the contrary, she is a cultured wife, mother and grandmother besides being a highly qualified academic. These qualities can be discerned in her chronicle of the mystical experiences that have befallen her.

These experiences focus almost exclusively on God the Father; and herein lies the main reason why Barbara Rose's book is so unique and, in a sense, pioneering, since relatively little has been written on special devotion to the First of Three Persons in God.

Inevitably, this subject-matter brings in to some extent the whole Trinity— that primordial and sublime mystery which can so easily mislead the unwary into theological error. But Barbara Rose is orthodoxy itself throughout these pages; she sees clearly that the Father is the first of the three co-eternal, co-equal Selves in the One Godhead, and that this Godhead is a Divine Family of Father, Son and Holy Spirit.

Because each of the Three is quite distinct from the others, we can relate to Them individually, that is, on a one-to-one basis. In this case it is God the Father who makes these amazing initiatives to Barbara Rose, favouring her through locutions with numerous revelations about Himself and His purposes.

These locutions could, in fact, be better described as dialogues, for the Father speaks not only about Himself and His plans but asks her questions. She in turn puts many a question to Him and voices her occasional fears and misgivings, addressing the First Person throughout with the candour and confidence of a trusting child.

What, then, is the Father's main purpose in holding these dialogues with Barbara Rose? Of what divine plan and initiative is she the chosen human instrument? The answer is that God the Father of all Mankind wants His paternal role to be more clearly and publicly recognized and honoured by all His human creatures. To this end, He proposes a Holy Octave of Consecration and an annual Feast-Day dedicated to Himself, plus a devotion known as the Chaplet.

In addition to being intimate and appealing, the actual dialogue throws much light on what we know about our loving Father in heaven. We sense the infinite tenderness and mercy underlying everything He says, while His favoured daughter comes across as full of filial trust and childlike directness.

The dialogue also vividly reflects the shifting moods of Barbara Rose's all-too-human spirit. Like the psalmist (indeed, like all of us), she experiences alternate highs and lows in her ongoing relationship with the Divine Being; one moment she is tip-toeing lightly on the mountain-tops of joy and consolation, the next she is wandering disconsolately in the valley of darkness and near-despair.

To return now to what was mentioned earlier: the book's power to stir our zeal for souls. This is because the Eternal Father tells us through Barbara Rose how immensely and tenderly He loves each of us human beings—His prodigal children though we are—and yearns to welcome us into His everlasting home beyond death's horizon. For example, Barbara Rose records Him as saying on different occasions: *"My children are precious to My Heart...They are My true desire...I long for them."* With such a price-tag on them, human souls are clearly precious beyond rubies. This is an inspiration and incentive of which we priests in particular stand in constant need.

A further item on the all-loving Father's agenda is: He wishes to unite the human family here on earth into a unity of harmony and brotherhood. Similarly He wants us to treasure as we should the unique gift He has made us of His Son's Eucharistic mysteries, the source of life and holiness.

What the Father likewise wants us to treasure as we should is His further gift of Mary, *"The Mother of all mankind."* He assures Barbara Rose that the Triumph of Mary's Immaculate Heart will be ushered in by the recognition of her privileged status in the meriting and mediation of grace.

The Mother of God has told Barbara Rose that she is preparing us for the *"Era of the return of the Father's children"* into His Paternal embrace. We have good reason to believe and hope that we are already standing on the very threshold of that longed-for era. Our Lady herself confirmed this happy expectation in another locution to Barbara Rose: *"Soon the Father will come to you and the world in a new way."*

In a word, Barbara Rose fulfils a prophetic role in preparing us through these pages for that brave new world wherein we shall pay a special honour and devotion to the First of the Divine Trinity. Over that approaching Age of the Eternal Father the Saints in Heaven, too, will surely rejoice—and none more so than the two great Carmelites who shared not only the name, Therese, but an intimate devotion to that Person referred to by Our Lord as, *"My Father and your Father"* (John 20:17).

Fr. Richard Foley S.J.
May 1, 1998

[Editor's note: Fr. Richard Foley's Foreword was written
for *Seeing With the Eyes of the Soul Volume I*]

INTRODUCTION

The author of this book, Barbara Rose Centilli, was 44 years of age when she began to record what she believed to be the voice of the Eternal Father speaking to her in prayer. Prior to this, her life was quite ordinary. Except for a few special experiences she believed to be of God, her life as a mother, grandmother, teacher and wife were typical of the average American woman of her generation.

Barbara Centilli grew up in a small town in Michigan and eventually settled after marriage in a midwestern state. After graduating from college, she attended graduate school and worked as a teacher from the late 1970's through the early 1990's. During this period she raised four children and became involved with research and educational projects for students with special needs.

Beginning in the mid-1990's, Barbara began to record in the form of a dialogue her prayerful conversations with God the Father, to whom she had developed a special devotion over her lifetime. These journals were eventually destroyed on the recommendation of a spiritual advisor who told her God does not speak to people in this manner.

However, in 1996, Barbara again began to record her conversations with the Father. By this time, she noticed God's responses to her in prayer were becoming very clear and distinct within her. She could hear His voice "in her heart and mind" and began to experience visions that sometimes accompanied the Father's words. Furthermore, as she reconciled and confronted what was happening to her, she became certain her experiences were not self-induced or imaginative but rather something she had no control over within herself.

It would not be possible to fully address the extraordinary contents of the revelations in this book. They cover a range of topics and are rich in detail concerning Barbara's interior life with God. Most of her reflections, resolutions and meditations are left intact, although some of what the Father granted to her for her personal spiritual edification has been edited out. This deleted material will eventually be published, as the Father has requested, in order to show, **"All My children what is possible with the Lord their God."**

However, the essence of *Seeing with the Eyes of the Soul* is unmistakable. The Father of All Mankind is requesting that through His Church all mankind be returned to Him. His home, He says, is all creation and His children must begin to come home to Him at this time. They must abandon any fear of Him and must know that He is all love, and all mercy.

The Father also tells Barbara that the end of an era is about to dawn upon the world and that these are truly prophetic times. Most significantly, the long awaited triumph of the Church is about to be fulfilled. This is the "Triumph" Mary promised at Fatima in 1917, and according to the Father's words to Barbara, will only be completely fulfilled in accordance with His will by His children returning to Him through two means: "personal consecration to God the Father" and by the Catholic Church proclaiming a "Feast Day" in His name.

While these requests appear to be separate issues, God the Father has outlined to Barbara a single process in which His children are to return to Him and at the same time honor Him with His feast day. Based entirely upon Scripture, the Eternal Father revealed to Barbara His desire for a special consecration to Him, known as *The Holy Octave of Consecration to God Our Father and Feast Day of the Father of All Mankind*. This consecration is based upon the traditions of God's people rendering Him honor and gratitude through eight-day feasts as recorded in both the Old and New Testaments.

Like in the days of old, the Holy Octave of Consecration to God Our Father is an eight-day consecration to be celebrated as a whole, culminating with a special feast day in the Church to honor the Father of All Mankind. The actual consecration involves a series of daily prayers, including meditations, a litany and the praying of a chaplet, all directed to God the Father.

It must be especially noted that the Father emphasizes to Barbara that there is to be no separation of the two - the Consecration and its Feast day. This is because, He says, the **practical purpose of the feast (day) is for My children to consecrate themselves to Me.**" The Father further states: "**The feast does not exist for the purpose of providing Me with a feast day on the Church calender. It is what the feast accomplishes — the return of My children to their Father! This cannot be accomplished with limited and temporary honor given Me at one Mass on one Sunday a year. No, this is much greater than one act. ... this is the final step towards the new era, a new relationship with their Father and God.**"

While much more could be noted, one final point is emphasized. Through the Holy Octave of Consecration and Feast Day, the Father declares to Barbara that this is the fulfillment of what was meant from the beginning. This, He states to her, is the meaning of the profound words in the Lord's prayer, **"Thy will be done ... Thy kingdom come on earth as it is in Heaven."**

Suffice to say, only after one reads this book can all its divine meaning, all its rich spiritual quality be understood. Men and women cannot be satisfied or content with anything except something greater than themselves - that something is our eternal God, revealed by the word of scripture, by the Catholic Church, and so often over the centuries by His chosen ones. *Seeing with the Eyes of the Soul* adds one more jewel to the crown of truth surrounding our creation and our Creator. Let us savor it and thank God once again for being so perfect in His awareness of our needs.

Dr. Thomas W. Petrisko

[Editor's note: Dr. Thomas Petrisko's Introduction was written for *Seeing With the Eyes of the Soul Volume I*]

2002

The Time of Times

January 5, 2002

This is my first night in my new home. As I reflect, I realize that what happened on Christmas was actually a present. Though it was so painful....

I have prepared a little sanctuary for myself—I can't see too far down the road, Papa. I am taking one second at a time and I ask that you guide my "every" step.

I am not clear on anything else yet, Father. And I have no idea what I am to learn from this or to teach others. I don't know yet myself. I look to my God and Church for direction and guidance.

Repeat after Me, daughter of My Heart—I am worthy of the trust given to Me by My Father.

Trust in what, Father?

To penetrate My mysteries. This is why I have chosen you.

Why?

Because doubtless you have many "doubts" about your own worthiness for this task; you have been emptied of self for this task. But now begins the work in earnest to go out into the world. And I ask you to tell them that I AM present now in this time and place—I am with you all—if only you would believe. Allow yourself to see and hear and touch Me in a special way.

Now go in My Peace and believe that I AM with you.

Reading: Is 17—..."Because though hast forgotten God thy Savior, and hast not remembered thy strong helper : therefore thou plant good plants, and shalt sow *strange seeds....the harvest will be taken away in the day of inheritance, and shall grieve thee much."*

January 12, 2002

I can avoid You no longer—in dialogue. I am in such turmoil, Papa.

You, little daughter of My Heart, are called to Love. Remain in My Peace—and Will.

Reading: 4 Kings 2:18—"*...Bring me a new vessel, and put salt into it....He went out to the spring of the waters, and cast the salt into it, and said: Thus saith the Lord: I have healed these waters, and there shall be no more in them death or barrenness."*

January 13, 2002

Dearest Papa:
It's as if something is keeping me from You. What is it? Why? I must almost force myself to write this, as if against some great counter-force. But I need to tell You I love You and that I am in tremendous pain regarding..... Why, Father, why? Help me to understand and to do Your Will. I am frightened— very frightened. Please help me. I need your help. I need You. I love You.

This, too, shall pass, child. And you will smile again. For a time, a very long time, you have come to Me with a sorrowful heart. And I have listened. But now I see a need for closure on an issue that has been as an open wound. And I lead you down a different path now. One which will never cease to amaze you with opportunities for love. You will pour yourself out in love for others. And you, too, little one, will know love. And this contrast will serve to model for all those who have eyes to see and ears to hear that God is good and I bestow My blessings on those who seek them with a pure and gentle heart.

You will know peace, little one. But you must pray more diligently in this time. I will never leave you. Bliss and happiness belong to those who seek their Father while here on earth.

Shalom.

Reading: Timothy 1:11—"*Which is according to the gospel of the glory of the blessed God, which hath been committed to my trust. I give him thanks who hath strengthened me, even to Christ Jesus our Lord, for that he hath counted me faithful, putting me in the ministry."*

January 14, 2002

Dearest Sweetest Papa:

I feel like my heart is breaking.

I feel paralyzed regarding Your work. Why? What is happening to me, Father? I feel as if my spirit and body and mind are dying. I am afraid.

Please grab hold of me, Father. I am too weak to reach out too far or too forcefully. Please, Abba, save me from my own self pity and exaggerated need.

Help me, please.

Yes, daughter, you have seen a great mystery. Ponder this in your heart and believe that I AM with you. You will find My words most pleasing to you.

Reading: Mt 15:21—*"And Jesus went from thence, and retired into the coasts of Tyre and Sidon. And behold a woman of Canaan who came out of those coasts, crying out, said to him: Have mercy on me, O Lord, thou son of David: my daughter is grievously troubled by a devil. ....Oh woman, great is thy faith: be it done to thee as thou wilt: and her daughter was cured from that hour.*

Thank you, Father.

January 20, 2002

Dearest Sweetest Papa:

I have found it very difficult to come to you in dialogue. I speak with you internally as I go about my daily business, but I'm having a difficult time concentrating on anything—prayer, movies, books.

I still don't feel physically well and though I was supposed to go on a retreat today, I didn't. I slept most of the day and feel ill.

My security, as it was, is gone and I feel very frightened.

I hope I heal this year. I hope I grow and put things into perspective. Help me to do that, Papa, please. That is my wish for this, my 50th year on earth.

Let me shine with whatever light You give me. I love You, Father, and I give myself to You.

[Then Our Father shows me the rocky sandy desert and I am in the part where my hand touches the earthen walls and I am lead to understand that this passageway where I am sandwiched in between earth lets out in a beautiful bright opening and this is the place of epiphany—and the cave, the Heart of God, the stars, and I am looking out from this cave with much peace. But I appear to be watching and waiting for something or someone. What can it be?]

It is I.

[And I am pointed toward the earthen passageway as if someone else will come through it.]

Barbara Rose, little daughter of My Heart. You have seen the image of one who waits for the great promise of when I AM to come among you in a new way. Revisit this image so it will become clearer. You are in My Heart and you wait to see another who likewise approaches My Heart—a like-minded person will come to you, who will have likewise found the way and you will both be with Me as I have ordained. Do you believe?

Yes, Papa.

Now treasure this moment of promise, for it will surely come. I decree such.

[I hear the word "passport."]

Shalom, little one, and remain in My Peace.

Reading: Tobias 13:10—*"Wilt thou kill me as thou hast already killed seven husbands? At these words she went into an upper chamber of her house: and for three days and three nights did neither eat nor drink: But continuing in prayer with tears besought God, that he would deliver her from this reproach. And it came to pass on the third day, when she was making an end of her prayer, blessing the Lord, She said: Blessed is thy name, O God of our fathers: who when thou hast been angry, wilt shew mercy, and in the time of tribulation forgivest the sins of them that call upon thee." [And God blessed her with her "eighth" husband]*

Believe.

January 24, 2002

Dearest Sweetest Papa:

Please help me. My reality, my paradigm of life has been upended and all the pieces that were my life are up in the air, and I do not know where they will fall. But this pain of rejection I feel is so painful....Show me the way, please. I need You and want Your reassurance. Thank you—I am listening.

Teach them to be kind and to love—fully in the Spirit of their One true God and Father. I must leave but I will return. You, little one, must take care to guide them in my stead in the Spirit of Truth, which springs forth from My Heart and is infused in each child who was conceived there. Do you understand?

No, not completely, Father.

I wish to leave a legacy with My children and this legacy is Love living in you and all those who hear and respond to My call in this time. Don't hesitate. Don't refrain from acting in response.

Tell them this—I will never abandon you—but I must go. There is much to do in the Great Battle that lies ahead.

But you will be safe. This I promise. And I will send those to you who need solace and encouragement in this theatre of war, and so it is in this time.

Believe, child. This is what I call out to you all. Believe in My Love that lives in you. For in this Love, I AM. In this love you reside in Me.

[Our Father takes my hand and I am led over a threshold. I lift my foot up and step over from a darker side into light—a beautiful bluish, crisp, clear light and I have a sense of a north land and spring—very slow, simpler life. And it is peaceful.]

You can open your eyes now and see what you couldn't see before—you reside in both the here and now and the future of possibilities. They overlay but are experienced in union.

I AM with you, Barbara Rose, smallest daughter of My Heart. Let Me in and I will never leave you. I will reside in the seat of Love, which is the Heart. There you will find Me—in every expression and experience of Divinized Love. Now be at peace, little one. And don't neglect your tasks regarding care of My small-

est children, bereft without the Special Presence of their Father. I remain, yet I must go for yet another time and in another way.

Say "Peace" and I will come.

Shalom.

Reading: Dt 15—*"In the seventh year thou shalt make a remission." [and begin a new cycle in the "eighth" year]*

January 28, 2002

Dearest Sweetest Father:

I miss You. I have been in the dark night—but yet I've always known you were here. It was never that you drew away from me as it was me being distracted away from You. And allowing myself to be carried on a current—and this current is mighty and powerful. I keep remembering what Fr.... said to me: (1) God knows what's best for you, (2) God brings good out of all things, and (3) give your Total Fiat. My life does seem to be quieting down. But it is always so full—and here I go again, complaining, always complaining.

Yes, things seem to be settling down into a rhythm. There is a truce, a peace, between...and myself. I accept... I will love...from a distance and accept—whatever your Will is for me.

February 1, 2002

Dearest Sweetest Papa:

Well, Father, we are having quite a snowstorm. Please protect all those people who are driving.

I am still becoming acclimated to my new surroundings. But I ache for my children and grandchildren and what could have been for our family. Please help me understand better. Guide me. Show me the way, please. I love You; I adore You; I worship You. I am listening, Father.

Tell ... of false horizons that mislead, disorient. Time is the great leveler and so it is that these days will see sorrow for choices misspent.

Now for all those children who are led to Me through your voice, I say this, little one of My Heart, duplicity cannot coexist within God Your Father's Heart with you, My Children. This cannot be. For one to exist within My Heart there must be a quieting of Spirit, a stillness, a clarity so that Truth may pass through unfiltered. The soul that is spotted blocks the Light and so Light does not pass through you from Me to others.

Understanding exists only with total abandonment in Love, a letting go, a gentle swoon of Heart, so that I may re-enliven the Heart with My own rhythm—so that two hearts beat as one.

This you will understand better in the days ahead. As I have always told you, no man stands alone, ever. You cannot separate Father from child. You are mislead, you who believe that you can exist without Me. For I AM Life. I AM your very Life. Sin no more, my little ones. Sin is separation from Life into Death.

[I hear the words "sun-bleached day."]

This is on the horizon, daughter of My Heart.

animus...dictum...potare

Shalom

Reading: 4 Kings 2:13—*"And he took up the mantle of Elias, that fell from him: and going back, he stood upon the bank of the Jordan."*

February 2, 2002

Dearest Sweetest Papa:

At last I am alone with You in the Adoration Chapel. It is a beautiful day. The bells are tolling, the sun is shining, and I am here alone with you in the quiet.

Although I am still experiencing grief and loss, I see Your hand in many things.

Barbara, do you hear Me, daughter?

Yes, Father.

Then write what I tell you. Sympathy for a system corrupted by greed is not salient. It is responsive to the needs only of those few for who it gains. Deci-

siveness is imminent—as the necessity for the tension to be released is great. I speak to you of a system, which exists in enormity on the earth. It is "one" system that permeates much. And what is this system, little daughter of My Heart? The system of lust. Lust is more than panting passion, one for the other. Lust is a coveting of something for one's own gratification—only. That is the only consideration. More, more—this is what drives the person who gives their soul up to lust.

Live for others, child, and you will do well. Live in Me and for Me alone. And in doing this, you will be loving yourself and all others because I AM with you and in you as a living Presence today and tomorrow—for without Me there is nothing—nothing.

When I design a true love, one for the other—it is with this in mind: that each gives their life to the other unconditionally in the image of their One True God and Father. To remove the child from the Heart of the Father is to kill the child for lack of sustenance and support. To remove oneself from the intimate bond of marriage, not through death, is to rip apart something that was not intended to be separated.

Now in this case, there is much bleeding, a hemorrhaging of the heart—but it will heal, little one.

Shy though you may be to ask Me if I Am addressing you, I will offer this wisdom: When we are in love, we do not examine the relationship from outside—we live it inside. This is what you have lacked, little one. Now I call you to praise My Name, Father of All Mankind, for the rest of your natural life on earth and ever after in heaven. And for this period of time that you linger on earth, I will guide you and protect you from the evil that waits at your door step to enter. But it will not because I AM with you for comfort and solace. And My ways are not your ways because I AM not alone. You, too, are in Me as I am in you.

Father, I'm sorry to keep complaining that I am lonely. Is this bad?

No child lives without the touch of another—it would be too cruel. All must be touched for a time. No, daughter, for you there is passion, emptying yourself for Me alone. Does this not please you, child?

Oh, yes, Father, but I am in such emotional pain and I am so lonely.

Shalom.

Reading: Phil 2:7-9—*"Who being in the form of God, thought it not robbery* *to be equal with God: But emptied himself, taking the form of a servant, being made in the likeness of men, and in habit found as a man. He humbled himself, becoming obedient unto death, even to the death of the cross. For which cause God also hath exalted him, and hath given him a name which is above all names: That in the name of Jesus every knee should bow, of those that are in heaven, on earth, and under the earth."*

February 19, 2002

On the 8th day of each month you shall draw near me in My Most Blessed Sacrament. I call you to this so that you might whisper in My ear, as I will whisper in yours, Barbara Rose.

All is suspended but for a time—and this sleep will revitalize you and strengthen you for the long road ahead. Have I not told you, Barbara Rose, that all is within My Plan and nothing will elude Me or frustrate Me?

I AM Who AM.

Tertio...Miserere...Corde

Reading: Gal 6:15-17—*"For in Christ Jesus neither circumcision availeth any thing, nor uncircumcision, but a new creation."*

May 8, 2002

Dearest Sweetest Father:

Oh, what a time this is....

[I'm seeing the river/boat image again. However, I can't see where this river is taking me. Strangely, now I can see the end—Your cave and You are in it—but I cannot see past the man with dark hair who stands in the river as my boat approaches. He is on one side of the river; my family is on the other. What does this mean, Father? What transpires past this point? I think I will have to rise up from my weakened state to actually see him. This man has been waiting and watching for the boat. He is very calm and peaceful and purposeful.]

Tell me, child, what it is you wish to see?

I guess I want hope, something to hang onto. I'm sorry, Father, but I am frightened, confused, and human.

Peace, little one of My Heart. Have I neglected you, ever? No, never. Not now, not ever. You see dimly the shadowy outline of your life—to be. But it remains incomplete as you have not yet made all your choices. These will be offered you in abundance—but you must always ask, "Whose Will be done?"

Yes, but this is a little thing in comparison to the last decision you will be required to make—this will be the most difficult of all—always for the greater good, daughter. Think, with which option lies the most probable good? Decisions should be made not out of fear of the law but out of love from the heart. If you love, you will not perish.

Your choice approaches, one which will determine your path hence forward. What do I want? I want you to love Me, love yourself, and all others—for I live within you, too, as you all live within My Heart. Love is dynamic, not static. It is active. Love will move you down the river you see, toward Me. But you must choose—to greet the one who has been sent or to seek those who appear lost to you. They are on the other side of the reeds—you, can still hear each others' voices.

I send the one who will approach you. You must choose.

Reading: Judith 8-13—*""You have set a time for the mercy of the Lord, and you have appointed him a day, according to your pleasure. But forasmuch as the Lord is patient, let us be penitent for this same thing, and with many tears let us beg his pardon: For God will not threaten like man, nor be inflamed to anger like the son of man. And therefore let us humble our souls before him, and continuing in a humble spirit, in his service. Let us ask the Lord with tears, that according to his will so he would shew his mercy to us: that as our heart is troubled by their pride, so also we may glorify in our humility."*

May 26, 2002

Dearest Sweetest Papa:

Here I am....

Peace, daughter of My Heart:

Lament no more. Fortunate are you who can hear Me—for I comfort you in your time of need. Trust is a difficult thing to measure, child. It is like the film of dew as it lies on the morning petal—sheer, weightless—but observable. And so it is with trust, little one of My Heart. I say to you, this—What one man decides is right and just, another might disregard. But what I decree is interminable.

It, too, is ephemeral, weightless—but the things that I declare as Truth must be maintained in the hearts of all true believers. And what is it that I have said: What I have joined together, let no man separate—no man. For as they are joined as one, separation would result in death.

You bleed, child, but for a time. And I will heal you, make you whole again. For in My future vision, you must be whole and intact. For I dwell in you and where I dwell all is made whole.

Cling to Me, little one. I AM real. I am your Protector, Father. And I AM pleased in your virtue and your trust in Me, not men. For in men you may be disappointed in your ideals but never with your One True God and Father.

Let...be for awhile and you will see such change as to amaze all those who doubted. Do not let go, even now. Have I not raised the dead to the living? Have I not restored life in those who were dead? Do not despair and do not harden your heart, child—little rose of My Heart.

Shalom.

Reading: Phil 2:17—*"Yea, and if I be made a victim upon the sacrifice and service of your faith, I rejoice, and congratulate with you all."*

May 30, 2002

Daughter of My Heart, My Smallest Rose:

You will not be happy in a worldly sense while you are alive on earth—but someday—soon—you will come to Me and all will be forgiven and forgotten [regarding......]

For it is as I have decreed—No love shall surpass your love for your one True God and Father. Love Me first—and all else will follow. Trust Me—and I will guide you.

Shalom.

Reading: Eph 3:14—*"For this cause I bow my knees to the Father of our Lord Jesus Christ, Of whom all paternity in heaven and earth is named."*

June 4, 2002

Dearest Sweetest Father:

I have become aware of something very upsetting in my family and I ask for peace in this regard. I am listening.

Draw near to Me, child. Have I not loved you? Listen to My Words to you on this night:

> *Trouble finds its way to those who look for it.*
>
> *Find your happiness in the small things of your life.*
>
> *These I give you in compensation for your trials.*
>
> *They will give you comfort for what lies ahead.*
>
> *A tremendous outpouring of Love is being directed at you now.*
>
> *Let it nourish you and sustain.*
>
> *I will appear to you soon—when you are ready.*
>
> *Believe in Me—*

Dona Nobis Pacem.

Reading: 2 Ptr 3: 9, 14, & 15—*"The Lord delayeth not his promise, as some imagine, but dealeth patiently for your sake, not willing that any should perish, but that all should return to penance....Wherefore, dearly beloved, waiting for these things, be diligent that you may be found before him unspotted and blameless in peace. And account the longsuffering of our Lord, salvation; as also our most dear brother Paul, according to the wisdom given him, hath written to you."*

June 8, 2002

Dearest Sweetest Papa:

I offer all the suffering of my.....to you. I hope that in some small way, it might help all people live out a healthy, spiritual marriage.

Please speak to me, Father, I am listening.

[I see a man, woman, and child in the woods. The man is pulling a cart—on which sits the woman and child. The man pulls the cart and the woman tends to the child. The man gets very, very tired. He stops and must rest.

The child has grown and now leaves the cart. The woman joins the man and they both begin to pull in tandem.]

Why do you show me this, Father?

I show you this so that you might believe that some marriages stop out of ill health or weakness. The man can no longer go on. He must rest—he must pause. Then, little one, the child who is no more goes off to find their own life and the burden lightened is much easier to pull. However, there are those who can no longer bear the weight—especially of sorrow—and so they let go of the cart. Some run, some rest. But always they remember that the burden was theirs. Does the woman cry out because she has been abandoned, her cart has stopped moving forward? No, she cannot, for to linger would be to die. She must continue on the journey alone, pulling the cart by herself so that she may rest and be protected and so that her children may accompany her on her journey at times.

[Could she not run off on foot, Father? As the husband did?]

Someone must carry the burden, which are the memories, the treasures of a family's heart, the home. Where is home? Yes, it is in the heart. But while on earth, you must live in the world. The man who leaves his burden—the family—always feels the pain, the loss, if only inwardly. Perhaps, though, daughter of My Heart, he watches from the bushes as his wife pulls the heavy load by herself and he may yet need shelter. Stay on the road—look straight ahead—remain where he might see you.

And you might sing and you might pray so that he is called to your voice.

Shalom.

Reading: Luke 22:48-53—*"And Jesus said to him: Judas, dost thou betray the Son of man with a kiss? And they that were about him, seeing what would follow, said to him: Lord, shall we strike with the sword? And one of them struck the servant of the high priest, and cut off his right ear. But Jesus answering, said: Suffer ye thus far. And when he had touched his ear, he healed him. And Jesus said to the chief priests, and magistrates of the temple, and the ancients, that were come unto him: Are ye come out, as it were against a thief, with swords and clubs? When I was daily with you in the temple, you did not stretch forth your hands against me: but this is your hour, and the power of darkness."*

July 8, 2002

Dearest Sweetest Father:

I am here before You in the Blessed Sacrament and I love You. I am listening.

Take what I give you as a gift, daughter of My Heart. This may be illusive—but always centered in Me—to which you will always have access, on some level—for you are in Me and I in you. As it should be with all good fathers and their children.

But I look to you in this time to define for My children who are so patiently waiting, what will be clarified in this time.

I AM your Lord God and Father. As a symbol of My Most Merciful Paternal Heart, I have given you so many gifts—each with a special purpose. Now you must glean from the dialogue thus far, all these presents from a Father to his children. Write them down and speak of them freely. Invite the world to meet Me in a new and special way for there occurs, even now, a rumbling, a movement which can no longer be denied and in this great and terrible rumble is a power to cleanse, to wash away the film, the residue of profane sacrifices—all for fruit that has been forbidden.

You will know of what I speak soon. But I AM with you and will never leave you, My children. You are Mine and Mine belong to Me.

I have said these things to you, not to frighten but to comfort you in the days ahead, hard and difficult days. For some will cry and some will shout for joy, but all will know that I AM God.

Shalom.

Reading: Is 15: 7—*"According to the greatness of their work, is their visitation also"*

August 2, 2002

Dearest Sweetest Papa:

I am so sorry. I get distracted. I am quiet now and I am listening—and I think that you want to speak to me—because I am here.

Peace, my daughter:

Liken what you are going through to a vise that is ever pressuring you from every side. This is so your soul—which is so precious to Me—may be purified and come to resemble more fully My image in you. For I reside where I AM welcome, dearest daughter of My Heart.

Now I take this time to tell you this—there will be moments when you will cry—die to self—and other moments will seem to bring you glory—but I tell you this—never are you closer to Me than in your suffering. Take this time to reflect on the purpose for this—suffering. What is the result—inside? Do you not better believe that I am with you? Only by comparison can you hope to see the light of My Son Jesus.

Take this time also to produce a work such as will reflect that Light out into the world—to all My poor children who do not know Me.

Be at peace, little one, and know I AM with you, always. Do not doubt, this, ever. The significance of this day will be manifested to you when you embrace the suffering I have given you—then you will understand.

Papa, what do you mean? Which suffering in particular? There are so many?

Dedicate your life to this—the education of God's children in their right as My sons, daughters, and heirs. They must know this so that they will not feel left alone in the last days of this time. The time of times, as I have previously said. Now do you see? It is for this reason that you have made ready the way of your Lord God and Father in these precipitous times.

Shalom.

Reading: Dt 11:10-17—*"For the land, which thou goest to possess, is not like the land of Egypt, from whence thou camest out, where, when the seed is sown, waters are brought in to water it after the manner of gardens. But it is a land of hills and plains, expecting rain from heaven. And the Lord thy God doth always visit it, and his eyes are on it from the beginning of the year unto the end thereof. If then you obey my commandments, which I command you this day, that you love the Lord your God, and serve him with all your heart, and with all your soul: He will give to your land the early rain and the latter rain, that you may gather in your corn, and your wine, and your oil, and your hay out of the fields to feed your cattle, and that you may eat and be filled. Beware lest perhaps your heart be deceived, and you depart from the Lord, and serve strange gods, and adore them: And the Lord being* *angry shut up heaven, that the rain come not down, nor the earth yield her fruit, and you perish quickly from the excellent land, which the Lord will give you."*

[I am made aware that this is the Pope of Our Mother [John Paul II] who now ushers us to her Son and from the Son to our Father. Two Popes after this one [there will be one who?] will embrace what the Father wants known to all His children—this: Love the Lord God Your Father with all your heart, soul, and mind for He enters you and will keep you within His Will.]

And this, child, is Heaven on Earth. [And I hear "His Kingdom Come—more fully."]

August 14, 2002

Dearest Sweetest Papa:

I see your hand in so many, many things. Lately, I feel as if I'm here but not here—one foot here on earth and one foot with you. Not completely engaged here on earth. I love you, Papa. And I miss our quiet times together—but I also know you have work for me to do—and I will do it.

I don't miss watching the news lately—it's so disturbing. I feel Your Presence so strongly—speak to Me, My Father, for I am listening.

Barbara Rose, Daughter of My Heart:

You sense My Presence and yet do you truly believe? I AM with you always. Not for a time, not for a moment—forever, forever.

Sometimes, child, I draw you close through suffering—it purifies your soul, as you know. But did you know, too, that these embraces of fire are by design? All is One in perfect conformity of action and movement. This is My Will—and this time of separation and seeming chaos—they, too, little one, are as if a force of erosion to shape and mold My Creation into the ultimate perfection that it IS—for I AM and all is in Me. Now go to your child, as I come to you—and believe.

Shalom.

Reading: Acts 17:24-29—*"God, who made the world, and all things therein; he, being Lord of heaven and earth, dwelleth not in temples made with hands; Neither is he served with men's hands, as though he needed anything; seeing it is he who giveth to all life, and breath, and all things: And hath made of one, all mankind,* *to dwell upon the whole face of the earth, determining appointed times, and the limits of their habitation. That they should seek God, if happily they may feel after him or find him, although he be not far from every one of us: For in him we live, and move, and are; as some also of your own poets said: For we are also his offspring. Being therefore the offspring of God, we must not suppose the divinity to be like unto gold, or silver, or stone, the graving of art, and device of man."*

August 16, 2002

Dearest Sweetest Papa:

I come to you today—to love you and adore you and worship you.

Listen to Me, child. Peace is here. Behold! I bring you the glory that is Mine through My Divine Son in this most Holy and Blessed Sacrament.

I tell you this. There will be no peace in this world until you address the problem which exists between God and man—you doubt Me, you neglect Me. So mournfully I call and call, My dearest daughter. My heart pines for the slightest touch of heart to heart—but it is lacking in this world made for and by man for no other purpose than to glorify man.

Can man have glory without God?

You are empty shells, child. Barren, barren, and the wind blows through; leaving from whence it came. You will not hold. You will not contain My Spirit because you lack faith and reason.

Where have you gone, My Children? Why have you wandered so far? Distance of the heart separates us. This and only this.

Now enveloped in the earth's sweet touch are the souls of the few out of so many who define the Light. This is their time—a new time to understand a gift yet hidden.

For this alone you have been saved from the flame that does not burn bright, but sputters, flickers a godless heat that is increasing ever. Do you feel it now, child? The signs? I have given you many signs. I have allowed many signs before your eyes so you may see....and be touched by My Heart.

I bid you Light, little one of My Heart. For the Light will save you all. Remember this.

Shalom.

Reading: 2 Pt 3—*""But the day of the Lord shall come as a thief, in which the heavens shall pass away with great violence, and the elements shall be melted with heat, and the earth and the works which are in it, shall be burnt up." Phil 4:7-19—"And the peace of God, which surpasseth all understanding, keep your hearts and minds in Christ Jesus....And may my God supply all your want, according to his riches in glory in Christ Jesus."*

The dawn breaks only after the sun has set on the horizon of your sight.

August 23, 2002

Dearest Sweetest Papa:

Quiet my soul. Please let me dwell on You more instead of all the activity around me. Quiet my soul, Lord. I love You with all my heart. I am listening, Father.

Spare the time, daughter of My Heart. Seek Me out whenever I call you. See Me in all that surrounds you. Hear Me in the voices that speak to you from My Heart. Let me remain with you throughout your days and remember that I have given you a great gift—the gift to bear witness to My all-powerful Paternal Love. There is no more potent Love than this. I lie in wait to capture your every thought. I lie in your heart—at peace, the peace I have given you for I have given you Myself.

Can your heart contain a love so great? No, daughter. It is not possible. But that modicum of My Heart that can penetrate your heart in the gentlest and yet powerful way, is, yes, contained there—the residue, the essence of My Love ever present—My Mark upon your soul, for you are Mine.

Now prostrate yourself before Me—for I AM the King of all that is—and true Father of Your Heart.

September 6, 2002

Dearest Sweetest Papa:

I love You with all my heart and soul and I grieve for all the hardness of heart and the disobedience of your children. And I am saddened by the attitudes of un-love and prejudice that weighs down so many people—even here.

Daughter of My Heart:

Truly today I speak to you, of what is yet to be known. What can this be, this thing that I wish to tell you? It is this, the outcome of the trial I have allowed for My children in the most gifted of nations, is a trial by fire. There will be a rain of burning heat that will descend so slowly but implacably on these, My dear strong-willed children. This fire will burn away the imperfections and the disease of want and poverty of Spirit which plagues you all.

Can I not trace your life on the horizon? Can I not know the everything of your existence? If so, then why do you think I cannot know the state of your souls— the dark, dark state of your souls. For you, the fire has gone out, unattended.

To rekindle this fire of the Spirit I will allow an exterior fire to allow you to see yourselves, to meet yourselves at last. There will be no more distractions of folly. Only grief for what was, but an increasing understanding of what should be. You must prepare for this desert of flame that will sweep over you in the days to come. But I will be with you always.

Remember, all things occur for a reason: from good comes good; from evil comes good. Do not forget this—it will provide comfort to you all.

Prepare, daughter. Shed all things unnecessary for earthly and heavenly life— for that is all there is—the rest is only illusion.

Pater...Omni; Deus...Pater.

Reading: Mt 6:11-13—*"Give us this day our supersubstantial bread. And forgive us our debts, as we also forgive our debtors. And lead us not into temptation. But deliver us from evil. Amen."*

October 26, 2002

Dearest Sweetest Papa:

Last night I had a dream and I was on the ground. The sky was grey and I saw a plane and somehow I knew it had someone on board who was well-known, a kind of celebrity, and the plane came in at a strange angle, lower and lower, and I knew it was going to crash, and I was horrified. I couldn't believe I was witnessing a plane crash.

When the plane came down it broke apart in pieces: wings, tail, and body and the body was like a box separated from the wings and tail. There was a man on board who was close to my age and he was slightly shorter than me. And somehow he was associated with something from the 60's.

[3:00 pm—I have just learned that Senator Paul Wellstone, his wife, and daughter, have died in a plane crash in Northern Minnesota.]

Papa, why did I see this plane crash last night?

Protect the innocent, Barbara Rose. I AM here in this moment to speak with you regarding the importance of "life." This cannot be understated. Life is the source of all that is—to deny this force from expression is to cause such ramifications as none of you, My children, can imagine. And it begins—the sequence of events that will lead to homeostasis once again.

All will settle into peace in My Heart, little daughter. Of this I tell you, remain in My Divine Paternal Heart. Here you will be protected. For it is here that you will know yourself and the Father who made you. You are Mine regardless of your ill-directed Will, a Will bent inward upon self instead of outward toward the source that sustains it. Do you see, Barbara Rose? Without sustenance from the Source the child dies. Will you willingly choose death, my children, over life in your Father?

Choose Life; choose Me. Love Me in the here and now so that you may love Me forever.

Shalom.

Reading: Mal 2—*"Have we not one father? hath not one God created us? why then doth every one of us despise his brother, violating the covenant of our fathers?....Because the Lord hath been witness between thee, and the wife of thy youth, whom thou hast despised: yet she was thy partner, and the wife of thy covenant. Did not one make her, and she is the residue of his spirit? And what doth one seek, but the seed of God? Keep then your spirit, and despise not the wife of thy youth?"*

November 5, 2002

Dearest Sweetest Papa:

I love You; I adore You; I worship you.

What a day, Father. So much happening—a day of decision in many regards.

But as with so many things, the battle is already won—we just don't see it or "believe" it yet.

What will happen with the Pro-Life issue in the election today? I love You, Father, and I wait for Your Will to be manifest. Please give me the grace to know and do Your Will. I don't even need to understand it.

The crisis that is around you ALL is the beginning of the event I have foretold to you, Barbara Rose. Relinquish what ties you have to somber logic and brief acquaintances and look beyond to what you cannot see—it is just this which I have given you as a lasting gift.

Speak openly of your love of the Cross. Why, smallest daughter? Because this is the Way, the Truth, and the Life—it bridges heaven and earth. Dying to self—

Have I not told you that these times would be difficult, indeed? They lack the luster and excitement of your previous years—they are desperate times, these which I have allowed.

So this I say—do not stop to tie your shoe or fasten your coat. Leave in haste for the safety of My Heart. Meet Me there for comfort. I will hold you close and whisper a sweet song of Paternal Love:

> *Deus Abba Pater*

> *Deus Abba Pater*

> *Deus Abba Pater*

Solemnity of My Divine Paternal Heart—

Say this:

My Father wishes such as this—a feast day commemorating his Fatherhood— in peace and good will. Love will bind us all. Love will heal the wounds so long inflicted on my victim children who serve in Love, in service to the poor and afflicted.

Let this be understood between us: August is the month of Me—Your Divine Father. Recognize Me for Who I AM. Am I not the Father of All Mankind? This day is to show the Truth about who you are and who I AM. This cannot be denied, for all know it in their souls, apart from worldly knowledge. You are in Me and I in you. My Heart is where you were conceived and sustained.

This is what I say to you—Love Me above all others and I will reside in you all— my tabernacles of Light in this time. Shine forth into the darkness for it descends quickly and you lack the time now to turn back the tide. It is upon you. Stay close to your Father. Do not stray. Come home, My children. Come home.

Shalom.

Reading: Dt. 12:13-17—*"Beware lest thou offer thy holocausts in every place that thou shalt see: But in the place which the Lord shall choose in one of thy tribes shalt thou offer sacrifices, and shalt do all that I command thee...and that thou wilt offer voluntarily, and the first fruits of thy hands."*

November 25, 2002

Dearest Sweetest Papa:

Life is very confusing. Sometimes I wish I could write the story of my life. But we aren't the authors of our own lives—You are. Someday I believe that I will be able to understand how I contributed to my own suffering. I'll see what Your Will was and how many times I didn't follow it or understand it or see it.

I just know I have this great gaping hole, this longing—physical, emotional, spiritual, intellectual. Every part of me aches for something I lack. I feel this great long sob inside myself that seems to exist just under the surface of my everyday life.

While I am here on earth, I have a longing for this that is distracting and overwhelming and over which I have no control.

November 30, 2002

Dearest Father:

I come to you today to ask for a great gift—the gift of understanding, acceptance, and peace.

Linger yet for awhile, Barbara Rose. Your eyes will truly be opened. Believe, little one.

Love Me, mind, body, and soul. Do not deny Me yourself for fear of the giving. I will not hurt you, child—only Love. Be at peace and remember, linger a bit longer and you will be given great insight into the problems of your years of suffering. It was not for nought—it was for a reason, graciously given, for your edification.

What would you have willed for Me, Papa?

Life in abundance—free to love, freely.

You will feel the pain for a time, but it will pass, little one of My Heart. It is being displaced by My Eternal Love for you and all My children.

Shalom.

Dona Nobis Pacem.

Reading: Rom 14:11—-*"For it is written: "As I live, saith the Lord, every knee shall bow to me, and every tongue shall confess to God....Let us not therefore judge one another anymore."*

December 3, 2002

All must be prepared for the great shift in perspective. For I will send it—mightily—and it will eradicate the chains that bind you all now. This was not My Plan but one that rushes ahead increasingly at a much more accelerated pace. Do you not know Me? I am here, little one, and wait for you to find Me—in your heart. Your presence here [Adoration] today pleases Me. Likewise, you will find that more prayer time will bring you ever closer. Believe in Me, little one. And see what unfolds before you.

Shalom.

Reading: Jn 1:23—*"I am the voice of one crying in the wilderness, make straight the way of the Lord, as said the prophet Isaias."*

December 24, 2002

Dearest Sweetest Papa:

How long have I been gone this time? My head swims in the requirements of my life.

Why, I wonder do such great traumas seem to occur around Christmas? I find that Christmas, which once made me so very, very joyful, makes me very sad—profoundly sad. Almost all semblance of a spiritual feast day are "almost" gone. You can barely see the religious reason anymore. Everyone is frantic, running around "buying" gifts. There is no speaking of God or of Love. Everyone is weary—so weary—and they hate what they do at Christmas, but they don't know how to stop.

My ... didn't want to put up a tree, listen to carols, be with family. Ours is a house of misery...My heart breaks. How can I make it better, Father? The example being given to the children.... And so again, I ask You for mercy for my family. Let them see the model I had as a child—of a Holy, Happy Catholic marriage and family.

[In a powerful dream I had a few years ago, I also experienced a Christmas where there was no tree, no celebration—and I felt panicky. I went out on a deck and looked out over the mountains and sky and saw signs or symbols, a kind of language or message written hugely in the sky. It was foreign to me; I didn't understand it. But what I did understand is that it defied all human explanation and was indeed evidence of God's existence and interaction with us—and I felt relieved, greatly relieved—but also very frightened. This Christmas reminds me somewhat of that dream.]

I love You, Father; help me to love You and my family better. Please. I am listening.

Shout, child, with love and joy, for it surrounds you! Yes, even now. For I have come in a new and cherished way. What is this way? It is love. Where love exists—there am I. This does not mean that a soul feels love from another. Rather, little one of My Heart, it means that you feel the love inside you for ALL others, regardless of whether that love is returned.

Place yourself in the view of your family—your loved ones and friends. Let them see the love you feel for Me. And I will come to them as well, because I AM with you and in you. When I reside in you, it is not you they reject, but Me, daughter of My Heart. They reject Me. So I ask you, do you grieve for Me or for yourself? I can bear this hurt, Barbara Rose—you cannot—without My aid.

Now I tell you this, what day have I given you for My Love to be celebrated? It is this Christmas and all Christmases, renewed each year in time. You see truly that the love enjoyed this holiday season is false— it is attached to things. Love is not things—it is a matter of the heart. We do not offer things in the place of our own hearts. This is not wise—with this practice, love of the heart wanes; it dies.

No, daughter, this is not the Way. I give you this gift for Christmas—belief and trust and love—these three are the foundation of all communion among My Children and in that I reside and am present.

Believe, little one, that the day will come when all will be made right in My eyes. You have only to do My Will—Love.

Reading: Sir [Ecclesiasticus] 7:12—*" for there is one that humbleth and exalt- eth, God who seeth all."*

Be Not Afraid.

December 28, 2002

Lay out the tent pegs, daughter. For soon the tent will be raised.

[I see myself on my knees hammering tent pegs into the ground—four. And this is under a large old tree and someone kneels down and motions to help me. I feel very comfortable with this person. And I hear the words, "Believe. It will not be long now. I will help you build a house that will stand strong and long—it will endure with our God's help." Out of his pocket, he hands me a melted red wax seal over a steel piece of metal, shaped like a large rectangular paperclip, or a butterfly—similar to the images in the Christmas sky. "By this you will know me. Wait for me, please."]

Reading: 1 Cor 14:3-5—*"But he that prophesieth, speaketh to men unto edi- fication, and exhortation, and comfort. He that speaketh in a tongue, edifieth himself: but he that prophesieth, edifieth the church. And I would have you all to speak wtih tongues, but rather to prophesy. For greater is he that prophesieth, that he that speaketh with tongues: unless perhaps he interpret, that the church may receive edification." 1 Sm 3:19*—*"And Samuel grew, and the Lord was with him, and not one of his words fell to the ground."*

December 29, 2002

[I see a special place of devotion to God Our Father—a simple home in the woods.] *And I will be with you there in a special way. And others will come for solace and comfort in the days ahead. A way station for travelers on their journey. And you will begin to believe again that I AM truly with you. Publish My words for the edification of others—it is so sorely needed. They must come to know that I have not abandoned my children. In your home you will place outside the door the heart I have shown you—the touchstone. Inside you will have the Cross with 8 candles and this should be lit for consecration prayers each evening. Soon the passing of one time into another will take place in your lifetime. And the shift will be painful and confusing. Do you deny this, little one? And so it must be for all things are transformed in the Love of your God and Father. I AM intense, but wearied by the inattention and rejection of My children. I can bear no more. Consecrate yourselves to Me, your One True God and Father—and I will protect you and keep you unto Myself, always.*

Come home, My children. I call you in this time of deep, deep darkness. Are you confused? Yes, it is so. These times disorient even the most learned. But the wise will recognize the signs and lean ever closer to My Divine Paternal Heart. Come to Me, little ones. I call you now. The storm, a mighty storm approaches, and I've come to lead you home.

Shalom.

Reading: 2 Pt 1:10—*"Wherefore, brethren, labor the more, that by good works you may make sure your calling and election. For doing these things, you shall not sin at any time; 2:4-6—"For if God spared not the angels that sinned, but delivered them, drawn down by infernal ropes to the lower hell, unto torments, to be reserved unto judgment: And spared not the original world, but preserved Noe, the eighth person, the preacher of justice, bringing in the flood upon the world of the ungodly. And reducing the cities of the Sodomites, and of the Gomorrhites, into ashes, condemned them to be overthrown, making them an example to those that should after act wickedly. Phil 2:1—-"If there be any consolation in Christ, if any comfort of charity, if any society of the spirit, if any bowels of commiseration: Fulfil ye my joy, that you be of one mind, having the same charity, being of one accord, agreeing in sentiment. Let nothing be done through contention, neither by vain glory: but in humility, let each esteem others better than themselves." John 15:27—"And you shall give testimony, because you are with me from the beginning."*

2003

THE TIME OF CHANGE

January 7, 2003

Dearest Sweetest Father:

I bought a beautiful Lady of Fatima statue. The priests here have given the statue a terrific blessing.

[I see 8 rainbows in the spring.] *Likely memories will return to My people in a pleasant, non-threatening way. It is time—the Day of the Eight Rainbows is upon you. It will be blessed by Me to show My children of what I speak—total abandonment to My Will. There is a reason, always a reason, for all that occurs. Do not forget this. My Will be done, little one of My Heart. In this be blessed—the sign of My renewed covenant with My children, all. The time is at hand for a transformation of hearts and minds and souls. In this believe—I AM with you always.*

Reading: Mt 20:29-34—*"And when they went out from Jericho, a great multitude followed him. And behold two blind men sitting by the way side, heard that Jesus passed by, and they cried out, saying: O Lord, thou son of David, have mercy on us. And the multitude rebuked them that they should hold their peace. But they cried out the more, saying: O Lord, thou son of David, have mercy on us. And Jesus stood, and called them, and said: What will ye that I do to you? They say to him: Lord, that our eyes be opened. And Jesus having compassion on them, touched their eyes. And immediately they saw, and followed him."*

January 19, 2003

Dearest Sweetest Father:

With the sweet there always seems to be bitter, too. There is no relief. Please be merciful, Father.

Your mission is clear, daughter of My Heart—pure and unceasing. Give yourself

27

to Me for My Purpose and My Purpose only—all else is but a shadow cast by your doubt. You imply that I have not heard you—yet I AM here. The path of peace is trod not by the learned but by those who dispose themselves to My Will. Having said this, have you not given yourself up to My Ordained Will? Then, smallest daughter, know that you are in My hands for My Purpose alone. Can you not guess at it? It is to Love with all your heart those I put into your life. It is meant for your own purification through trials—so many trials. But in the end, daughter, you will triumph and your soul will be clean. For you are Mine. Now be happy.

Reading: Jn 3:15—*"That whosoever believeth in him, may not perish; but may have life everlasting."*

February 3, 2003

Dearest Sweetest Father:

Our Lady has prompted me to begin again—and so I will. And I will begin again by listening. She says I am to cry out (against all "errors of heart"—the lack of love or loving the wrong things and for the wrong reasons). This, she says, is the crime for which we will be convicted and found most seriously guilty.

I do not doubt these words and wonder why there has been such a lull in the dialogue—why my heart and mind have been numbed. But I give myself again in full consecration to My Father—and I am listening, Father.

....

Footprint of the Lord—to follow—it is clear why do we hesitate? Why do we hold back? Why do we resist? Is it because we lack the courage or resolve? Then we must look up, extend our hand and he will pull us up and gently lead us home where our Father awaits us, tirelessly and without end.

Jesus, please help me. Do we not see? Do we not hear? The time has come for a reckoning—all must answer for the wrongs of this world. And we watched, passively, as the lamb was slaughtered—and cried and whimpered—so innocent—so blameless—so unprotected. We must cry out in this time that all wrongs must be addressed for the good and glory of our Lord, God, and Father.

He takes delight in our smallest effort. He draws ever nearer to our hearts— where he lives in each of us—though inhospitably in so many. We must treat him better. We must love Him as He loves us, so tenderly—and in loving each other we love Him Who lives in all His children. For it has been said, "Those Who lack resolve will be strengthened and these who lack hope will be given much in the ways of mercy."

Thanks be to God.

Anno Domus Pacem.

Reading: Ex 7—*"And Pharoh's heart was hardened, neither did he hear them, as the Lord had commanded. And he turned himself away and went into his house, neither did he set his heart to it this time also."*

February 7, 2003

Dearest Sweetest Papa:

I love You; I adore You; I worship You.

The world seems to be on the brink of war and terrorism. Sometimes I feel numb—as if in a bad dream. But this is real. I wonder if it is possible that Our Lady's Last Message at Fatima (3rd Secret) refers to those things that have not yet come.

Please listen, daughter—

Place all trust in Me, Your Lord God and Father. The future looks bleak. But it is the desert...remember? And what waits for you on the other side? First, you must follow your dear Mother through the harsh and dusty terrain. And she will lead you to the lush green, living near the water's edge where the boat which is My Church will carry reinforcements to you—those great men of the Church— apostles to renew a Church reborn in the Spirit so that all may begin again. Near the lake—that is where they will approach you, these men of Mine, to show you the way of Life in this new era. Open the book, daughter, and find Me there.

Reading: Dn 5—*[Daniel reads and interprets the handwriting on the wall]...."and thou hast praised the gods of silver, and of gold, and of brass, or iron, and of wood, and of stone, that neither see, nor hear, nor feel: but the God who hath thy breath in his hand, and all thy ways, thou hast not glorified....thou art weighed in the balance, and art found wanting."*

February 11, 2003

Dearest Sweetest Father:

So much danger in the world and it is spiraling out of control. Please, Father, help us to love one another. I ask that "You" intervene in our history in a most evident and powerful way. Let them see, Father, that we are one family and that you are our Father. Father, Your children misbehave and they need You to discipline them, so they learn humility and obedience to Your Will—most importantly, to Love You and each other. But could you please help us—we bungle, we make mistakes, we are selfish and immature. Father, I love You and I give myself to You. I am listening—

[I keep seeing something from the perspective of being inside a window and there is someone glowing with God to my right and we are looking out—and the glow is out there, too, and it is beautiful and good. It's as if I'm seeing this from sort of vehicle that is moving, like perhaps a train. And I see a circular, semi-circular satin, buttoned/tucked settee and babies are to go there, but I do not see them yet and I cannot see what this settee surrounds, but it does—some type of throne, statue, etc. And I now see a baby and it lies with its head to my left side and it is facing me and looks at me and I am knee-level to the baby's eye level. And I hear the words, "And it was good."

Dona Nobis Pacem.

Reading: Rev 8 [the seventh seal is opened] **& 15** [those that have overcome the beast, glorify God; the seven angels with the seven vials]

February 18, 2003

Dearest Sweetest Papa:

You know what is in my heart. The disappointment, the frustration—and the desire to do Your Will in all things.

[I hear, "Prepare for the troubles," and I see a bright light come out of this place in "20 + 10 years." I think this means we will suffer for the next 30 years (2033), but then some sort of miraculous white Light will burst forth from here. I'm certain I will be gone by then.

The world is in horrible disarray and I don't see a way out right now. I think

I would like to remove myself and live a quiet, peaceful life away from all this craziness—but I would miss my family.

The old sadness of heart is setting in. It does not frighten me. I know it will pass. What can I do for You, Father? The smallest thing.

This time of working is different from my time at home, with all the quiet. My relationship with You has changed. It has been more through people. And I accept this.

The desire to love is strong and I see You in so many people. I think this is the Martha cycle of my life. I had the Mary cycle and I believe I will have it again, someday—but now is for a different purpose.

[I see Our Lady and she is on her knees on the floor—sitting back—and rocking and distressed and she says, "***Peace, Pray for Peace.***" And she has on a multicolored tapestry, dark colors. And I don't know what to do for her, but I try and feel what a mother must go through whose children are going to harm each other. The family is falling apart—this insane world is affecting "her" family. The Father must come home; he needs to get involved for sanity to come back. And the children must feel fear and anxiety, and trepidation, and pain to deter them from the free fall they're in. Father should come so our Lady doesn't cry so much. Papa, please come and intervene before something terrible happens.]

Reading: Is 14:32—*"And what shall be answered to the messengers of the nations? That the Lord hath founded Sion, and the poor of his people shall hope in him."*

February 25, 2003

Dearest Papa:

I had the strangest dream last night, vivid. It was at the place where I work and a poor, foreign child had eaten some type of nut from a tree in the West. This child said she put it on cereal. In these nuts was some kind of wormy parasite that infected her. And there was no way to get it out of her. And you could see that she was in excruciating pain—horrible. And there was talk that she would be "euthanized." And it almost seemed like a merciful thing to do. And this thing produced "9" by-products, similar to the original nut, that multiplied every hour/day? And if consumed/breathed could infect someone else. And I helped care for the child but was also concerned that someone else in my care would become infected and have to die. The wormy parasite was this thing growing and getting bigger inside her—and there seemed no way to separate the two so the child could live. And I asked about her parents, but the nuns said they were taking care of her.

Father, is this an important symbolic dream?

Child:

The house is immaculate. It has been cleaned and readied now for My children to inhabit this home I have created.

In 9 days there will be a rumble unlike any before in the world. The innocent must sacrifice life so the horror that has grown, feeding off the innocent, cannot go on to infect others. This is different than any of the previous plagues that have befallen My people. Likely, it will be missed if it is not indicated as such. But it exists—it is in your midst. You have only to look and see. The child perishes, is dying, killed for the sake of so many who "can" be saved. This is the undaunted truth, little one of My Heart. So it shall be as I have shown you.

[I am made aware of a separation of good from evil.]

Reading: Gal 5:12 & 17—*"I would they were even cut off, who trouble you.... For the flesh lusteth against the spirit: and the spirit against the flesh; for these are contrary one to another: so that you do not the things that you would." James 3:12*—*"Can the fig tree, my brethren, bear grapes; or the vine, figs? So neither can the salt water yield sweet."*

March 8, 2003:

Dearest Sweetest Father:

I have come to you on the eighth day of the month....As soon as I come to You—"I love You; I adore You; I worship You" comes to my mind and across my lips—without any thought at all. I know you must have put them there.

And, Father, I continue to pray that you guide me—very, very closely. I am full of conflicts. Oh, Father, define me—please—this haziness is terrifying.

Listen, My Child:

Empty yourself of all that bothers you. Do I not hold you in My Divine Paternal

Heart? Cradle you in My hands? If this is so, why do you question or wonder?
I am always with you.*

But, Father, what if I don't listen to You? What if I make a big mistake?

*Have I not raised you up so you might see better? Have I not trained you Myself?
Have I not walked with you through every crisis? Every doubt? Yes, daughter,
I have done this and more. Now please see this—*

[I see that I am standing on the deck of a ship. I see the grey metal, and I
am looking out, and I see the Statue of Liberty—only the ship is going out
to sea, not in to land. And it is very foggy. I hear "We can no longer remain
here to survive. We must leave so that we might return—home?" Then I
hear, "Move to the forward deck," where it is the murkiest and foggiest. I
only know we are leaving the familiar, the symbol of freedom.]

Oh, Father, what are you showing me?!

Respond, daughter of My Heart.

[I see that I am alone on the deck, and I am hanging onto the metal support
framing on the side deck (doorway? overhang?). And I don't feel afraid
because I know My Father is with me.]

*Delight in this grace, little one—and you will remain free...to see Me through
the eyes of your soul. Call Me and I will move ever closer. Peace, child. Now
kneel and say this prayer:*

> *I will remain with My Father forever.*
> *Bathed in the sweet Mercy of His Divine Paternal Heart,*
> *Rooted as a babe in its mother's womb,*
> *Suckling for sustenance from My Father's own Spirit.*
> *But I am free in the universe of My Father's Love—*
> *There alone am I free—*
> *For I choose My Lord God and Father. Amen.*

Reading: **1 Pt 3:4**—*"...But the hidden man of the heart in the incorruptibility of
a quiet and meek spirit, which is rich in the sight of God."*

March 18, 2003

Dearest Sweetest Papa:

The earth moans. There is a sense of anticipation, of dread, of relief, of fear, as the War in Iraq approaches. We can feel the current of consequences pulling us closer and closer to the edge. In one sense, we are terrified and resist what is to come. In another, we embrace it, hoping that there will be a cleansing, after which will be hope and goodness, simplicity, and light. But along with this is a sense that to get to that point, we must go through fire and devastation and loss of loved ones—and we are terrified. The paralysis and lack of control we feel as we hang suspended over the precipice of this inevitable conflict is numbing, anaesthetizing.

However, Father, there is such a sense of "seeing" things more clearly—right and wrong, good and bad. And that also contributes to the uneasiness and grief—the apprehension, the revulsion. St. Paul said we now can see only through the glass darkly—but I believe that is changing somehow. The darkness through which we see is becoming thinner, is dissipating.

And it is everywhere on every level, in every culture, community, and family.

"You will no longer behave badly," I hear, applied to each situation. Enough is enough. The cup runs over. And Our Lady cries and cries—as we cry over what will be. Oh, Father, please have mercy. Soften the hearts of those who are cruel and hurtful. Let Your Will flow through us please. Let it blow through us. Let it overtake us. Let us lie down in Your Will and be carried to where you want us.

I love You, Father. Please help me be a good daughter. I am so imperfect. So imperfect.

Show us the way, Papa. We need You. We need You to come home and put your family's house in order. Our Mother is crying and Your children are running wild! They need their Father's firm but loving hand. A mother does not have the heart to inflict pain. A mother's heart is designed to love tenderly. A father's, though, demonstrates expectations—for the child's own good. And a father is capable and willing to do whatever it takes to save that child—even by pushing that child away so he/she can feel the consequences of not listening to their father's advice. But the father always hopes—

The death knoll rings for the unjust and the unforgiving. For they would not come home. Prepare, little one of My Heart. In increasing waves, shall My Will wash over the earth near you, over you, and in you. And you shall be saved the darkness of this day. Be at Peace.

Reading: Mt 21:6-15—*"And the chief priests and scribes, seeing the wonderful things that he did, and the children crying in the temple and saying: Hosanna to the son of David, were moved with indignation."*

March 25, 2003

Dearest Sweetest Father:

I saw a covenant rainbow bend to earth and in the middle of it I saw the Pillar of Fire from Exodus rise up toward the sky. And our beloved Jesus was in the center. This was during the family rosary last Sunday night. And just now before the Blessed Sacrament I was taken back [in my mind] to the room of the altar and throne and I came before our Father and He said, "This war must stop," and I was puzzled because the evil in Iraq was so horrible. And I asked, is this a just war, and he said, "It is just."

It was meant to prepare the world for the announcement. The Passion is upon you all—all My Children. Be purged now, My little ones, of your sins. Deep within your souls is a light, flickering in the darkness which has been this world and soon the darkness will no longer effuse [allow any] light. No, it will instead be as murky as the waters of the deep, deep sea. And it will swallow those who have allowed their light to cease, who have not tended to the flame of faith, hope, and love. This is the only way—the light that lives within you.

Punishment is a strong word for what takes place now in your life times. But it must be for the sake of the whole world. Be purged, My children, of that which makes you sick—sickened to death, mortal and spiritual. For these vices will be washed away in the maelstrom of the deep, deep darkness which in its chaos will be sucked down to the lowest depths of hell.

The Path of Peace lies ahead of you, clear and bright and open. The doors to this peace have been flung open wide; you have yet to step upon this path, the stones that line the way. And do not fear, little ones. All is fulfilled in My Time and My Good.

Reading: Mt 11:17—*"But whereunto shall I esteem this generation to be like? It is like to children sitting in the market place. Who crying to their companions say: We have piped to you, and you have not danced: we have lamented, and* *you have not mourned." Jn 14—"Let not your hearts be troubled. You believe in God, believe also in me. In my Father's house there are many mansions. If not, I would have told you: because I go to prepare a place for you. And if I shall go, and prepare a place for you, I will come again, and will take you to myself; that where I am, you also may be."*

I see our Father on the Throne in the room again—and He says, "Temporary."

April 8, 2003

Dearest Sweetest Father:

I come before you in Adoration today to ask for Your help in getting me back on track with my life. Please show me the way. I only want to do Your Will.

What do you see, child? What do you see?

[I am looking at the Black Madonna and the mottled golden background and vaguely I can see images but my first reaction is not to bother, it is too difficult—and then you prompt me to LOOK and REALIZE and TRUST, and that it is all right. I see someone kneeling on the ground. I see Our Lord hunched over (flinching) with the crown of thorns on His head. I see an old prophet, ecstatic, communicating with heaven. I see Our Lord with His eyes closed and He is, I believe, dying on the Cross.]

I bless you in your choices, for they are Mine, living in you. Believe and be at peace.

Reading: Mt 10:11-21—*"And into whatsoever city or town you shall enter, inquire who in it is worthy, and there abide till you go thence. And when you come into the house, salute it, saying: Peace be to this house. And if that house be worthy, your peace shall come upon it; but if it be not worthy, your peace shall return to you. And whosoever shall not receive you, nor hear your words: going forth out of that house or city shake off the dust from your feet.....Behold I send you as sheep in the midst of wolves. Be ye therefore wise as serpents and simple as doves.....for it is not you who speak, but he Spirit of your Father that speaketh in you."*

This can no longer be a culture of death. Our Father is Life.

This is the time of change—be prepared and trust!

April 9, 2003

Dearest Sweetest Papa:

I'm sorry I come to you late tonight. You know the reasons. I am taking a room nearer to my job and getting a small puppy. Father, I ask that you are with me every day. Please guide my steps—and I pray for the crisis in the Middle East. Father, I love you—totally. And I am listening.

Listen, daughter of My Heart, and learn:

When I come to you, it is with blessings—for I bless all My children abundantly—but you do not see.

Why?

Because, little one, you look too intently at that which goes counter to My Will.

But is this the intended focus? No, never—it is love, love of a Father for His children, all.

I bequeath to every child a deep abiding sense of the spiritual, of the mystical—it is inherited—from Father to child.

I look upon you all—those who love in humility and those who reject out of cruel selfishness—with a fondness born of a love that IS. It is eternal.

Yes, you breathe, you experience, you live in this world I have created—you experience My Creation and you experience mankind's effect on My Creation—this is an act of co-creating, walking in the Father's steps. But this modeling [relationship] is not always perfect—it is flawed as you have much development that is yet to be finished.

Rest in this knowledge tonight: this world is illumined with My Love in every moment—you have only to see with the eyes of your souls and hear with your hearts—My Kingdom Comes on Earth as It is in Heaven.

Dona Nobis Pacem.

Reading: Ex 30:6—*"And thou shalt set the altar over against the veil, that* *hangeth before the ark of the testimony before the propitiatory wherewith the testimony is covered, where I will speak to thee."*

May 5, 2003

Dearest Papa:

While praying the rosary I was with our Mother under her cloak and she was walking toward the sun and there were other children under her cloak. And we were walking and she was gathering us close and said, "Talk little and learn much." And then I saw the side profile of Our Lady, when Jesus was in her womb, and I knew that I was seeing something important and overlayed on top of this image I saw St. Catherine of Sienna's fish within the ocean and I was led to understand that the image of Our Lady carrying Our God inside of her—two separate humans, yet in one body—two but one—one but separate—that I understood this was the physical manifestation of a spiritual truth so that we would understand the concept of the Trinity and of Christ within us. And I asked where was the Holy Spirit and it was the Life force that was pumping through Our Lady, keeping her alive but then channeled into the baby where it was the same but different. All three needed each other—all three—though the baby proceeded (would proceed) from the Mother. And then I saw the Father's Divine Paternal Heart in Our Mother's pregnant side profile.

Now I understand more fully why Life is sacred, why pregnant women are "special." Why mothers are special—they are the outward appearance of a Divine Truth.

And women give life for those [men] who cannot. We are interdependent in this way, female and male. But men must do their part—protect and cherish and love the woman and the eternal life she gives him through their child.

The Divine reborn into this world, temporary, changing in time, in time to change.

Shalom, little one of My Heart.

Reading: Micah 2:9—*"....you have taken my praise for ever from their children."*

May 20, 2003

Dearest Sweetest Papa:

Things feel hectic again. I can't catch my breath with all the activities. Why can't I ever catch up, Lord? As some wise person said, "It's always something." I wish I could stay home.

I thank you for the newly expected grandchild in our family and I consecrate this baby to You and Our Lady, as I do all My children and descendents to the end of time. And, likewise, backwards, for all those who preceded me. That's what is so great, Papa—with you all things are indeed possible.

Outside in; inside out. The Kingdom is within us and is manifested outwardly. Intersecting realities; created realities. God enlivens all reality. He exists in all realities, all times, all places. He is the Divine Constant, the Eternal Constant. Everything else is fluid and in flux.

I love You; I adore You; I worship You. I am listening.

Read Genesis 15. Peace be with you, daughter of My Heart. Shalom.

1 Now when these things were done, the word of the Lord came to Abram by a vision, saying: Fear not, Abram, I am thy protector, and thy reward exceeding great. 2 And Abram said: Lord God, what wilt thou give me? I shall go without children: and the son of the steward of my house is this Damascus Eliezer. 3 And Abram added: But to me thou hast not given seed: and lo my servant, born in my house, shall be my heir. 4 And immediately the word of the Lord came to him, saying: He shall not be thy heir: but he that shall come out of thy bowels, him shalt thou have for thy heir. 5 And he brought him forth abroad, and said to him: Look up to heaven and number the stars, if thou canst. And he said to him: So shall thy seed be.

6 Abram believed God, and it was reputed to him unto justice. 7 And he said to him: I am the Lord who brought thee out from Ur of the Chaldees, to give thee this land, and that thou mightest possess it. 8 But he said: Lord God, whereby may I know that I shall possess it? 9 And the Lord answered, and said: Take me a cow of three years old, and a she goat of three years, and a ram of three years, a turtle also, and a pigeon. 10 And he took all these, and divided them in the midst, and laid the two pieces of each one against the other; but the birds he divided not.

11 And the fowls came down upon the carcasses, and Abram drove them away. 12 And when the sun was setting, a deep sleep fell upon Abram, and a great and darksome horror seized upon him. 13 And it was said unto him: Know thou beforehand that thy seed shall be a stranger in a land not their own, and they shall bring them under bondage, and afflict them four hundred years. 14 But I will judge the nation which they shall serve, and after this they shall come out with great substance. 15 And thou shalt go to thy fathers in peace, and be buried in a good old age.

16 But in the fourth generation they shall return hither: for as yet the iniquities of the Amorrhites are not at the full until this present time. 17 And when the sun was set, there arose a dark mist, and there appeared a smoking furnace and a lamp of fire passing between those divisions. 18 That day God made a covenant with Abram, saying: To thy seed will I give this land, from the river of Egypt even to the great river Euphrates. 19 The Cineans and Cenezites, the Cedmonites, 20 And the Hethites, and the Pherezites, the Raphaim also,

21 And the Amorrhites, and the Chanaanites, and the Gergesites, and the Jebus-ites.

May 28, 2003

Dearest Sweetest Father:

I thank you for all the people in my life, and I ask that Your Will is done in all their lives, as in mine.

Show me the way, Papa.

I have lost the way.

I want to come home now.

I have wandered long enough.

Take the scales off my eyes,

Let me hear Your voice,

Let my heart beat again,

Let me touch Your face.

For I would know you once again,

as in the past,

were it not for the distractions.

So many little things.

But all for You—

Slow down my life, Father.

Let me be at peace.

My soul is restless.

My heart is bleeding.

Someone has to put their finger in the dam or it will overflow—

the tears.

And wash over me and all around me like a tidal wave.

Seal my bleeding heart with the fortitude and efforts of the One and only One.

And this One must be Me—your God.

Let Me seal this wound

Let Me put My finger into your wounds—

Empty, lonely, hidden from the world.

And My finger will spark once again,

This Life I gave to you so many years ago.

Lay Me down and let Me rest now in your heart,

And let Me dwell in your chambers forever,

Daughter of My Heart.

Reading: 3 Saying:— *Hurt not the earth, nor the sea, nor the trees, till we sign the servants of our God in their foreheads (Rev 7:3).*

June 3, 2003

Let go, daughter of My Heart. You may let go now. Have peace in knowing that your tried. But all is as it is and cannot be changed, no matter how well-intended. No, little one, this has played itself out and you are left with a decision.

This chapter is closed. Move with the tide and let the current move you to a new place, loving and kind—know and teach about the Path of Peace, My Way of Love, so all can see and believe.

There is a polarization so that forces may be drawn together. To be drawn together, they must be pulled apart. The farther the distance, the stronger the eventual pulling force. And when they collapse into one another there will be no more hate or ugliness, only love and beauty will triumph over evil and evil will cease to exist because it has been subsumed, overtaken by My Love.

Let go, tiny rose of My Heart—open your hand and let the bird fly. Trust that your love is a beacon that will draw those to you that are meant to be drawn. Only then will you realize the strength I have given to you.

When you allow....to [hurt] you, you are allowing ...to [hurt] My Presence in you.

Repentance is only one part of the homecoming—desire and need is the other. Desire to love and be loved. Without that there can be no homecoming. The soul is lost.

Shalom, little one of My Heart.

Reading: Psalm 44—*"And the glory of the king's daughter is within in golden borders...."*

June 15, 2003

Dearest Sweetest Father:

I don't know if I'm made for such a complicated and chaotic life. How would you have me live out the rest of my life?

Please speak to me; I am listening.

Believe, daughter, in what you cannot see. I hold you even now. Come to let

Me in your heart—and behold, a new beginning. Trust Me. I will lead you in ways that are everlasting and peaceful. And My joy will remain with you all the days of your life. One more day. That is all. Try and remain in this image. Rest upon My tender and merciful breast, waiting upon my Word. Trust and be strong.

Reading: Dan 2—*[Daniel, by divine revelation, declares the dream of Nabu-chodonosor, and the interpretation of it.]"....Then was the mystery revealed to Daniel by a vision in the night: and Daniel blessed the God of heaven, and speaking he said: Blessed be the name of the Lord from eternity and for evermore: for wisdom and fortitude are his. And he changeth times and ages: taketh away kingdoms and establisheth them, giveth wisdom to the wise, and knowledge to them that have understanding. He revealeth deep and hidden things, and knoweth what is in darkness: and light is with him."*

July 12, 2003

Dearest Sweetest Papa:

I love You; I adore You; I worship You. I have been away so long. Where? I really don't know—only the sense that I couldn't write to you. Why? I don't know. It's not that I lost my faith. It was as if this cloud of anesthesia had surrounded me, as if I am in constant action and not contemplation. There is a tension in my family right now—the looming specter of death. A cherished family member may suffer very much and die—just as a new little life is coming into our family. Life and Death; death and life.

I've told my family members that this world is not all there is and that death is nothing to be afraid of—the best is yet to come! And kiddingly I said that whoever gets home to Our Father first has to have dinner ready for the rest of us when we get there.

Dither of My Heart:

There is a lesson in all this, an end to the suffering. But if you could see. The line between heroism and senseless self-destruction is fine, very fine.

What do you see as your life goal now that time has passed?

The same—very little changing.

But Life is in flux and change, always. Mark what I say to you now. The road is steep, very steep, little one, and the incline is such that you cannot possibly see what lies on the other side.

Believe. Have faith that all is transformed into good through My willing hands.

Reading: Phil 5:11—*"Let your modesty be known to all men. The Lord is nigh.....I speak not as it were for want. For I have learned, in whatsoever state I am, to be content therewith."*

ONE FORETOLD MOMENT

January 8, 2004

Dearest Sweetest Papa:

I come to you today in front of the Blessed Sacrament to ask for your merciful guidance with a matter of great importance. I have been hiding from myself and You and now wish to approach You with love and trust. I only want Your Will to be done in my life. I am listening, Father.

Your speech leads you to Me, daughter of My Heart. But it can only take you so far. What is it you truly seek? Is it peace or comfort? Is it ease of mind? Or do you seek Me out of Love—to be with Me in this short hour? I am delighted that you have come, but I ask you again—why do you seek Me?

I want the pain to go away.

But, little one, the pain will not go away until you seek Me once again out of Love. Satiate yourself with what I offer you in all times, all places—Myself. Does that not satisfy?

Father, I am shackled in this place of pain and can think of nothing else until I feel some relief. I am human—

And yet divine—for I live in you as I dwell in all those children that recognize Me as their One True God and Father.

You are free now from what has oppressed you, but what now will you do with the life I have given you? Will you seek Me still once your pain is gone?

Yes, Father, I give myself to You. Do with me what You will.

This is what I wish, little daughter of My Heart—believe that what I have planned for you since the beginning of time will be—

What, Father—I just want to "know."

That you reside with Me in your heart and share Me with your brothers and sisters. Forgive, daughter. This will save you. But remain in My Peace in this way—pray ever more that what exists above is clearly seen on earth and that what is below is clearly seen as such on earth—the imperfect physical manifestation of a Kingdom of God, outside My Kingdom.

Know this, Barbara Rose, when My children deem the time appropriate to look no more for succor from the world of their misguided making, they will see Me, as I have always been here—just a fingertip away, within reach, but unacknowledged. You cannot see what is above if you do not look up. Do not look down, and I will visit you all in My Time in your hearts. This is greater than you realize—much greater. See with the eyes of your soul—and tell ... he stands at the threshold of a great work. The door is cracked, now he must choose to open it into a greater light of understanding. He will remember what I say. Think not of yourself but of those who have need of Me—soon.

[I hear "Be not the Earth but your Father's heavens always within your heart."]

READING— *I was exceeding glad, that I found of thy children walking in truth, as we have received a commandment from the Father. 5 And now I beseech thee, lady, not as writing a new commandment to thee, but that which we have had from the beginning, that we love one another. 6 And this is charity, that we walk according to his commandments. For this is the commandment, that, as you have heard from the beginning, you should walk in the same: 7 For many seducers are gone out into the world, who confess not that Jesus Christ is come in the flesh: this is a seducer and an antichrist. 8 Look to yourselves, that you lose not the things which you have wrought: but that you may receive a full reward. 9 Whosoever revolteth, and continueth not in the doctrine of Christ, hath not God. He that continueth in the doctrine, the same hath both the Father and the Son (2 Jn 4—9).*

January 15, 2004

Dearest Sweetest Papa:

I feel more and more exhausted. I think I could sleep around the clock. I know I have many people and things pulling on me—and yet I should not be this tired. I feel as though I am literally slipping away, as if the very life is being drained out of me. I don't believe it is depression; I think I am dying—which we [humans] all are. But I feel rather close to death, being pulled faster and faster.

It's almost peaceful, a letting go, a letting, Father. I feel as if my job is done here on earth and I can let go now. I hope this attitude is all right with You. I hope I am not being a coward or a quitter—or selfish. I am just so tired—and I want to go to sleep. I am listening, Father.

Daughter?

Yes, Father?

Can you hear Me?

Yes, Father.

Do you love Me?

Yes, Father.

Then begin to trust that all is well with you and do not concern yourself with what you see as death. Every moment is well spent when it is spent with Me— your One true God and Father. Breathe deep, child. Breathe in My Spirit that emanates from My Heart to Yours—filling you with Life.

What you crave cannot be. For you have yet to do much for My Glory. This entails increased attention to My Divine Paternal Heart. It is there you rest, little one of My Heart. You are but resting in your Father's heart.

Sleep, little one, and be renewed. Apostasy is afoot and growing ever closer to where you lay your head [intellect?]. This is True—you are never alone when you rest in My Divine Paternal Heart.

Taste this sweet dew of heaven before the coming of the high noon sun. From the sun all things grow—but from the sun some will perish from the searing heat and light. But you will be resting in the shade of My Heart, drinking deeply of the dew of heaven on earth.

Shalom, little one of My Heart.

READING:—*4 Who gave himself for our sins, that he might deliver us from this present wicked world, according to the will of God and our Father: 5 To whom is glory forever and ever. Amen. 6 I wonder that you are so soon removed from him that called you into the grace of Christ, unto another gospel. 7 Which is not another, only there are some that trouble you, and would pervert the gospel of Christ. 8 But though we, or an angel from heaven, preach a gospel to you besides that which* *we have preached to you, let him be anathema. 9 As we said before, so now I say again: If any one preach to you a gospel, besides that which you have received, let him be anathema. 10 For do I now persuade men, or God? Or do I seek to please men? If I yet pleased men, I should not be the servant of Christ.*

11 For I give you to understand, brethren, that the gospel which was preached by me is not according to man. 12 For neither did I receive it of man, nor did I learn it; but by the revelation of Jesus Christ. 13 For you have heard of my conversation in time past in the Jews' religion: how that, beyond measure, I persecuted the church of God, and wasted it. 14 And I made progress in the Jews' religion above many of my equals in my own nation, being more abundantly zealous for the traditions of my fathers (Gal 1:4-14).

March 20, 2004:

Dearest, dearest Papa:

I have been in the desert for so long. Last night I had an experience, one of those that are indelible. I am in the boat—with Jesus—and He is paddling down the river (guiding the boat). And it is summer and for some reason I am always at the head of the boat, lying down, my eyes peeking over the edge, and I can see the beautiful river water—clear—and it is green (full of life) and I let my hands skim across the water, and I can feel the sun above and hear the summer sounds and smell summer.

This time, however, I somehow had fallen out of the boat and was splashing around and Jesus pulled me up (it reminds me of the fountain/well scene at the top of the valley) and what strikes me is I don't know how I got out of the boat, but the way I was flailing around I think I was shocked and frightened. And this time I looked at Jesus and he looked at me, so kindly, and I didn't want to look away from him—even to see where we were going.

I'm sorry, Jesus; I'm sorry, Father, if I have been too distracted by my surroundings and they have pulled me into the deep water—and I didn't even realize it.

I am feeling very stressed. My blood pressure is up and I'm having too many incapacitating headaches—too many hats, too little time. May Your Will and only Your Will be done in my life. Let me know what that is and give me the wisdom, courage, and fortitude to do it. I miss you, Papa. I miss the quiet times with you. Please help me be a good daughter. Please. I am listening.

[Jesus] **You bend the truth.**

How, Jesus?

You need to give your "assent" to your "yes"—a freely given "yes," given in love and total abandonment. Will you do this at last?

Yes, Jesus. I will. Please help me. I am so weak.

Tell ... that he believes he has been abandoned by the One Who seeks him out. He cannot hide—no, little one of Our Father's Heart. He, the one who must be told, is waiting for this word in patience and aggrieved submission. He, too, is learning of My Way—remember it is not what may seem to be successful in man's eyes—but in Mine and My Father's, your total abandonment and devotion are such a small offering for the graces gifted to you both. You must once again in earnest tend to the mission you have been given, tenderly and with much love. ... will know. He is My mouthpiece in this regard. Learn to listen and submit to those I have given you for My great purpose and that of My Father's— a return of His children home to their One True God and Father—of Whom I AM the Son Who has saved you all—from yourselves, in spite of yourselves, because you are so beloved by the Heart of the Trinity that beats unceasingly in rhythm and harmony, the music of Love, audible to all those who will hear and believe in these grave times.

Yes, I have reminded you again of the realities of this time. It is lethal, little one of My Father's Heart and Mine. This you cannot escape—the darkening sky and high winds that approach from the East. Look to the East for your chastisement and Salvation—it is near—both separate and yet the same. Contained in one foretold moment—a clap of thunder—and then you will know and believe that what I have told you has come to pass. But this is so, not to frighten you. Always what is allowed to come to pass is for good in My Father's eyes—the good of His children, all, whether they acknowledge Him or not. But that time soon approaches and will not remain hindered much longer—time bends back upon itself—ponder this, Barbara Rose.

My Peace I give you.

Reading: Matthew 11:14—*"And if you will receive it, (J) he is Elias that is to come. He that hath ears to hear, let him hear.*

J) [Reference back to the Book of Malachias] "Behold I will send you Elias the prophet, before the coming of the great and dreadful day of the Lord."

April 28, 2004:

Dearest Sweetest Father:

Father, guide my steps and protect me in my choices. Help me be a good daughter to You....I am listening to you, Papa.

[I see two high rocky surfaces, side by side, and they are being smacked together and they are turning into power. And the two rocks are spread all over the United States, sparkling, like gems.

And it was good.

What is good, Father?

The collision and annihilation of two hearts side by side for My Light to shine. Both of you have your trials, daughter—both. Both is fixed in place. Let me repeat what was said, if you think that what is present to your earthly eyes and ears—and that this is reality—then you are missing the nuance of the whole of My Will. My Will, little one, is woven intricately through all that was, is, and will be. You see only the pale shadow of what is. To comprehend the Divine Design you must be transformed in My Spirit and then you will see all things new. Is this not true, even in your own life—now!

Remain but awhile in your present state. Do not suffer yourself over those things which you cannot comprehend fully for you are still in the flesh and must remain so until the work I have given you has been completed. Soon you will see a stupendous change in what has been. The world will know that the end of an era is upon it. But a new one, smallest daughter of My Heart, begins—and you will see it in its infancy only—but you will see what is to come, and you will know that My hand is upon the world.

Now sleep, daughter, and know that all is within My Will. This should give you comfort. I love you, Barbara Rose.

Shalom.

Reading:—*And the people went forth, and brought. And they made themselves tabernacles every man on the top of his house, and in their courts, and in the courts of the house of God, and in the street of the water gate, and in the street of the gate of Ephraim. 17 And all the assembly of them that were returned from the captivity, made tabernacles, and dwelt in tabernacles: for since the days of Josue the son of Nun the children of Israel had not done so, until that day: and there was exceeding* *great joy. 18 And he read in the book of the law of God day by day, from the first day till the last, and they kept the solemnity seven days, and in the eighth day a solemn assembly according to the manner. (2 Esdras 8:16-23)*

April 29, 2004:

Dearest Papa:

My heart cried today. When will the pain stop? Help me, Father. I am listening.

[I see across a stream into the wood and there is a beautiful gentle green light filtering through the trees—it is gorgeous. I hear "Remonstrance." But I don't really know what it means. Our Father also leads me to a clearing and there was a circle of rocks, a fire pit—and Our Father told me, *"It is only sensations, only sensations. Pass on this truism: Fate waits for no man or woman—it is as established in My Will. Ponder this freely and often. Your lives were, are, and will be."*

Why does my heart cry, Father?

It breaks for love—it is broken, but not lost. See that light and let it give you the peace you need.

Shalom.

Reading:—*4 Desiring to see thee, being mindful of thy tears, that I may be filled with joy. (2 Tm 1:4)*

July 25, 2004:

Dearest Sweetest Father:

I am not "feeling" my Faith and this condition is or has been worsening....I fell off the path, got lost, but I want to rediscover the path again. But I need Your help in whatever way you want to give it. May Your Will be done.

[I find myself beneath the sea with Our Father. I was lead by the arm gently by a tall angel and we recited the Our Father prayer together. I asked Our Father why we were under the sea, and he said to better know him and that I should write this down:

    The Cross Face to Face

The Daughter approaches the Father for her right.

Spiritual children—

The Fiat.

The right of the espoused,

The promise—

The covenant—

Unbroken

Where all those dwell in the heart with

God in the Sacred Place.

He Heals.

[I live under and above the water with My Father—in two worlds.]

Shalom, little one of My Heart.

Reading:—*And Tobias took hold of it and drew it from his eyes and immediately he recovered his sight. (Tobias 11:15)*

October 4, 2004:

I can't think straight....I'm curled up in a ball of pain and I don't know how to make the pain stop.

Barbara...Barbara

[I turn away and don't want to listen.]

Father, why have you abandoned me?

How can I help you when you won't let Me?

How? What else can I do?

Act in your life. Am I not wiser? Am I not more potent?

The pain only gets worse. How can this be help?

"Rectify"—all must be rectified first. Then you will see the sense of it. Doubt this and you doubt Me, daughter of My Heart.

Rectify what? I don't understand.

Make straight the way of the Lord, for He comes to you.

How?

By believing that I am with you and within you, working in ways that you cannot know.

Why?

Because, little one, you are blind to so much but you will see and believe all I have said to you.

What do You mean by "rectify," Father?

To make right the wrongs, to fill all that is darkness with light. How do you right a wrong? By forgiveness and mercy.

It is too much for me. Too much. It is not that I choose not to. I can't.

Then you must lean on Me. Hold onto Me. I won't leave you. But know this. If you believe that from all bad can come good through the love of God, then you will have begun to heal.

That is too easy an answer, Father, too general, too vague. Father, help me please.

Be reassured that the choice is yours and it will be pleasing in My eyes, if it is done without malice and in love and forgiveness and for the good of you all. You guide the ship now, daughter. And it is in a mighty storm. Will you continue to steer it into the maelstrom or toward Peace? Where is Peace, little one? Where are the seas blue and calm?

I don't know!

Toward the shore. Toward land. Toward home.

But where is that?

You are in the home and heart of your family now. Make your home bright and comforting and strong so that it can weather the storm without. You are the heart of your family, the heart. And the heart must continue to beat strong and steady—no more unnecessary exertion. Protect your heart. Protect your heart, little one. And I will bathe it in grace and light and goodness. Treat it well.

Shalom.

October 31, 2004:

Dearest Sweetest Father:

Can someone be so lost that they don't realize they're lost? I have no excuse except to say my foundation has been severely rocked. I have felt very little except to keep going, going....always trying to catch up. So many things....

But I always knew I couldn't hide forever.

And so I am here tonight to begin again, on this eve of all saints.

Much of what I have believed has been put under fire—

I just want to be quiet with You before I go to sleep tonight and ask for your mercy and forgiveness for my neglect of You. I am not worthy, Father.

[I am in a barn—turn-of-the-century farmhouse—and I am little—maybe 10, maybe 8. And I am on a bicycle that is in a stand. It's a bit too big for me. And I'm peddling madly—it's out of control and I'm not going anyway. Finally, I'm frightened and I get off and I take the bike off the tracks and wheel it outside into the sunshine. I begin to ride it down the road and I'm balancing and I'm moving. And I'm controlling the pace and then I fall into the gravel and grass. And I get hurt, but it's like I'm anaesthetized. And I cry,"Father, Father," and He comes out the front steps of the white farmhouse and picks me up and pats me on the back to comfort me. And He says He's the strongest daddy in the whole world and nothing will hurt me—He'll protect me. And then He says my Mother wants to see me. And I smile when I see her. She is in a rocking chair and I sit in her lap and the rocking becomes too fast and it feels like the bike in the barn. And I think

I'm supposed to remember what it felt like and I'm frightened and pray the Our Father several times and the rocking slows.

Then my brother [Jesus] comes down the stairs and I smile and he goes and sits at a round wooden table in the same parlor. And I crawl under the table, hand on the intricately carved pedestal. My mother gets down and crawls under with me and she is comforting. And Joshua looks under the table and I see my Father standing there but He doesn't get down. And then He goes and sits in a big arm chair and looks upset. And somehow I know it's over me. And then I also realize I am clinging to the wood for my life—and it's the Cross. And I know if I let go, everything will be out of control, spiraling out of control.

My Mother is with me under the table top. Jesus is still bending down. My Mother is at my side. And they all seem a bit concerned. And I know I have to hang on tight to the wood and visit here much. There is much to learn. And I hear my Father say,

Placate Me, daughter. Remember I am with you always—there is none—no one—who can take My place. Now rest where you are. Soon this storm of confusion will pass. You will recover if you remain here in the home of My Heart. Spend time with Me and you will regain My Peace. Remain with Me, daughter. Time is short but I AM eternal—always, forever.

Shalom, little one of My Heart. And now it is All Saints Day. Regain your strength. Breathe—breathe in deep of My Spirit—and we begin again, little one of My Heart.

Reading:—And they sung together hymns, and praise to the Lord: because he is good, for his mercy endureth for ever towards Israel. And all the people shouted with a great shout, praising the Lord, because the foundations of the temple of the Lord were laid. (1 Esdras 3:11).

December 8, 2004

Dearest Sweetest Papa:

I had an "experience" during Mass on Sunday, after receiving the Holy Eucharist, that was very beautiful. I was in the boat with Jesus and I turned around and looked in His eyes and said, "What do I do now, Jesus?"

Then I saw a polished wooden box lined with red velvet and in the box, right to left, a gold ring, a staff of life," and a red rose. The Staff of Life (I heard the words) is a wooden branch with delicate green leaves and tiny white flowers near the top.

Then I saw myself in the boat with Jesus again. And we were facing each other. Our arms were raised upward, our hands together in prayerful position toward Our Father in Heaven—on observation, I realized this created a triangle.

I'm uncertain about the items in the wooden box. I have no clear idea what they mean.

The staff—it is alive, blossoming—but only a part of something larger.

Reading: —*4 Be not as your fathers, to whom the former prophets have cried, saying: Thus saith the Lord of hosts: Turn ye from your evil ways, and from your wicked thoughts: but they did not give ear, neither did they hearken to me, saith the Lord. 17 Cry yet, saying: Thus saith the Lord of hosts: My cities shall yet flow with good things: and the Lord will yet comfort Sion, and he will yet choose Jerusalem (Zach 1:4, 17).*

Time Bending Back Upon Itself

February 15, 2005

Dearest Sweetest Papa:

What a changed person I am....different. I don't believe I could have kept this change at arm's length. It came upon me in an overpowering rush and left in its wake an unnatural calm, a deadness, a lack of emotional feeling. I survive now. I breathe, I eat, I go to work, I take care of my family responsibilities—but my heart is lifeless.

I do not hear, I do not see with the intensity I did for so many years.

I don't wish to begin this long overdue dialogue with personal life questions. I have learned that the path I go down in this life is one I must journey on alone—sometimes feeling Your Presence, sometimes not. And that the purpose of these dialogues is not for You to tell me what to do or what will happen—although I've begged enough for this very thing many times.

I wish I could be a better, happier, more energetic person. But as much as I try to push my body and mind and soul—I can't, at least not alone.

Despite my seemingly dead heart, I find myself many times saying, "Help me, Father—please help me...I'm lost." And even though I'm not "feeling" anything and even though it seems that you're not responding, just my ability to mumble, "Help me, Father," keeps me connected to You in a strange, obscure way.

When I see a baby, I smile. When I see a puppy, I smile. It is brief and the smile comes without any conscious effort on my part—and it lets me know that "something" good is still operating somewhere in my cloudy brain and silent heart.

This, I hope, is a start again of my conversations with You. Even if You choose not to speak to me; even if my heart cannot hear You. It is a start, a new beginning. Most of all, I do want You to know I love You, even though I haven't been able to "feel" love for so long now. My love is a choice and I am sorry that I cannot feel it. But I know You have enough love for both of us—for everyone, for all times, for eternity.

So the lack of feeling of love is my shortcoming, not Yours. And I will try very, very hard to endure it, this loss, without letting go of the life-line I have that I pray connects me to You. And I ask You, even though I know I don't deserve it in any way, that You not let go of me, give up on me. Because then I will really be lost—then I wouldn't even be able to move my lips to mouth the words anymore. I really have need of You—always—but in a special way now.

[I have just encountered Our Father for the first time in awhile and I felt so unworthy, and I had a difficult time hearing and seeing Him. This is what I experienced: I heard, "Do you want Me to help You," several times, but I could not see Him.

Then He said for me to feel His love and I must love His Son. He told me to give Him all that burdens me—but that He wouldn't take it away, only I must join it to Jesus and His sufferings. And I took this to mean that perhaps I would just spend the rest of my life suffering. But He said *"no"* (though I am in almost constant bodily pain now). Our Father said that I have a story to tell yet—that is my mission. And that the story was about His love for His children. And I thought He meant some historical account and that I have no real scholarly knowledge of that—but he immediately said, "You are a blank slate on which I will write My story." And then He became smaller and more distant and I felt I was coming back into my body or away from where I was. And He said, "Peace be with you—Shalom."

He also asked me if the Apostles hadn't sat with their Lord God Jesus and, despite this, didn't they leave Him and run away? And I thought about it and said, "Yes," and then I realized He was trying to help me not hate myself so much—because I did. As I was leaving Him, he said, "Do not hate yourself, daughter, for you are Mine." He took a ring off His finger and placed it on mine and it was gold with blood red rubies. And that is all I remember.

Reading: —*11 Persecutions, afflictions: such as came upon me at Antioch, at Iconium, and at Lystra: what persecutions I endured, and out of them all the Lord delivered me. 12 And all that will live godly in Christ Jesus, shall suffer persecution (2 Tm 3:11). 11 A faithful saying: for if we be dead with him, we shall live also with him (2 Tm 2:11).*

February 16, 2005:

Dearest Sweetest Father:

What am I doing wrong that there is no time left in a day? Even the busiest lovers have (or make) time for their beloved. Sometimes re-arranging their lives. But what if obligations keep you from that luxury? I know I must be doing something wrong, and rationalizing it by thinking I'm loving You by keeping my obligations to family and work is not reason enough. There has to be a better way, a different way—but what?

It is 12:40 am (at night) and You are the last thing I get to. Teach me, show me. Please. I am listening.

Barbara, are you there?

Yes, Father, I am listening.

Continue to listen to My voice despite the distractions that plague you. Listen and you will know that what is imminent is by Order of My Holy Will.

What do you mean by "imminent," Father?

What comes to you all now, yes, even now before recognition formally occurs.

Formally, Father? What comes to us all?

Do you not see? Can you not hear? Have I taught you nothing of worth in these years. As I draw from sight, from sound, from hearts, in a special way, there is a void, a vacuum, which nothing will be able to fill. This hunger will be most painful, an aching as yet known by My children.

I withdraw so that you may see and may hear and may feel and may come to understand that He Who Is with You Always has been hidden from your view. I have spoken of this to you before on previous occasions, daughter of My Heart. You must know that I will never leave My children, never abandon them—but the veil has been imposed for "a time and a time" for which there will be no remedy. You will look, but you will not find. You will listen, but you will not hear. Why? For retribution, punishment? [No] For justice's sake My children's choices have demanded that this separation take place so that a reunion, a rebirth may occur. Each has their own measure of light within their hearts. This is the result of My Grace and each child's response. Some lights are stronger, some dimmer than others. And now in this Period of the Veil of Eternal Justice, you will be barred from the intimacy, which has been cultivated in this past century through My Most Beloved Son, Carol, John Paul II, the earthly Father of My Church.

Father, how long will this veil hide You from Your children?

No more will I tell you, daughter. Yours is to know that this darkness and oppression you sense is the result of so many choices made, more quickly they are made in a world that is now run mad by humanity's indifference to all that is good, all that is Sacred.

And now when My children look, they will see themselves reflected. My image will not be smiling back at them with compassion, mercy, and Paternal Love. They have brought down the Veil once again, as in the times of Old, times past, ancient times, when I was separated from all but those chosen by Me.

What will happen to us?

You will live as you choose but without the special graces I have showered—but that have been refused these many years. And now the results, My Little Ones. I beg you to fan the flames that remain in your hearts before the veil blocks out all light, My Light. For then, little ones, you will have only the lights in your own hearts to guide you in these treacherous times.

Barbarism in the most monstrous proportions is visiting you and still you cannot see your fates. Life without your Lord God and Father is Death in disguise.

Father, please help us. Help the whole world. I don't know why everything is so "monstrous" and "barbaric," but how can it be stopped, turned around. Please help us.

You ran away from the Truth and the consequences of Touching the Light of Truth. You are safe, daughter of My Heart. All those who seek Me with earnest hearts will not be lost in these times. Recall, I spoke of time bending back upon itself and so it will, until My children have cultivated not only knowledge—but Wisdom—and that only through the Father Who Loves you all.

One day, daughter, I make this promise, love will permeate this world I have created and it will last for generations. But My children are far from love. And now they must ponder evidence of their loss as it will be shown to them in increasing ways.

Shalom, Barbara Rose. Rest in My Peace.

READING:—*1 God created man of the earth, and made him after his own image. 2 And he turned him into it again, and clothed him with strength according to himself. 3 He gave him the number of his days and time, and gave him power over all things that are upon the earth. 4 He put the fear of him upon all flesh, and he had dominion over beasts and fowls. 5 He created of him a helpmate like to himself: he gave them counsel, and a tongue, and eyes, and ears, and a heart to devise: and he filled them with the knowledge of understanding.*

6 He created in them the science of the spirit, he filled their heart with wisdom, and shewed them both good and evil. 7 He set his eye upon their hearts to shew them the greatness of his works: 8 That they might praise the name which he hath sanctified: and glory in his wondrous acts, that they might declare the glorious things of his works. 9 Moreover he gave them instructions, and the law of life for an inheritance. 10 He made an everlasting covenant with them, and he shewed them his justice and judgments. 11 And their eye saw the majesty of his glory. and their ears heard his glorious voice, and he said to them: Beware of all iniquity. 12 And he gave to every one of them commandment concerning his neighbour. 13 Their ways are always before him, they are not hidden from his eyes. 14 Over every nation he set a ruler. 15 And Israel was made the manifest portion of God. 16 And all their works are as the sun in the sight of God: and his eyes are continually upon their ways. 17 Their covenants were not hid by their iniquity, and all their iniquities are in the sight of God. 18 The alms of a man is as a signet with him, and shall preserve the grace of a man as the apple of the eye: 19 And afterward he shall rise up, and shall render them their reward, to everyone upon their own head, and shall turn them down into the bowels of the earth. 20 But to the penitent he hath given the way of justice, and he hath strengthened them that were fainting in patience, and hath appointed to them the lot of truth. 21 Turn to the Lord, and forsake thy sins: 22 Make thy prayer before the face of the Lord, and offend less. 23 Return to the Lord, and turn away from thy injustice, and greatly hate abomination. 24 And know the justices and judgments of God, and stand firm in the lot set before thee, and in prayer to the most high God. 25 Go to the side of the holy age, with them that live and give praise to God. 26 Tarry not in the error of the ungodly, give glory before death. Praise perisheth from the dead as nothing. 27 Give thanks whilst thou art living, whilst thou art alive and in health thou shalt give thanks, and shalt praise God, and shalt glory in his mercies. 28 How great is the mercy of the Lord, and his forgiveness to them that turn to him! 29 For all things cannot be in men, because the son of man is not immortal, and they are delighted with the vanity of evil. 30 What is brighter than the sun; yet it shall be eclipsed. Or what is more wicked than that which flesh and blood hath invented? and this shall be reproved. 31 He beholdeth the power of the height of heaven: and all men are earth and ashes. (Sirach/Ecclesiasticus 17).

February 19, 2005:

Dearest Sweetest Father:

How are You? I am listening.

[I hear our Blessed Mother Mary]: ....*I will tell you this as your Mother who loves you so tenderly. Believe in the God Who made you, Who longs for you and all His children. This is how your Father is, was, and always will be—a good and loving Father. Waiting for you all—this is His wish, as you know, and could only fully understand through your talks with Him. He speaks and you should listen. This is what I ask of you. Listen. He will call you in times when it is most beneficial for your dialogue. Be open to His voice. Trust these callings. They are from the Lord God, and Father of us all. I remain with Him but come to you in your times of need. Listen, Barbara Rose, and He will call you. Yours is to listen and write so that others may benefit from the goodness which comes only from the Lord God Our Father.*

Mother, how will I know when he is calling me, especially when I am so frantically busy almost all hours of each day? Sometimes this seems almost impossible.

It is no longer for you to decide the time and place. He will come to you—you need only to say, "Yes," and withdraw into quiet.

Mother, is there some way I can know for certain that He is calling and wants me to drop everything to listen? What if I'm watching my grandchildren, or driving, or teaching? Or with a group of people?

You will be lifted up in Spirit in times chosen by Our Father. He is all knowing, but also wise. Is he not, daughter?

I am speaking to you now in such a state. Can you not feel it—as you did on the night previously? It is sleepless sleep or so it seems, a sweet dream for one such as yourself, to be with Our father in such a personal dialogue. It is good that you disallow yourself full acknowledgement of this experience. It is a tender mercy allowed you by the One Who loves you.

The call will be clear—there will be no doubt and these calls will occur at times when you can say, yes, yield, if it is your choice. This is what I have come to tell you in this special night. Look on the calendar and see its significance in the Church year. I am your Queen and Mother—and always close by when you have need of me.

[After looking this day up, I'm not certain if it is February 18th or 19th to which Our Lady refers. This dialogue was written, starting at 12:54 am. The 18th is the feast of St. Simeon (Simon) and the 19th is the feast of Franciscan hermit, Conrad of Piacenzo—or in the ancient Roman Catholic calendar, these two days would have been Lenten "Ember" days.]

READING:—*15 And again he said: Spread thy mantle, wherewith thou art covered, and hold it with both hands. And when she spread it and held it, he measured six measures of barley, and laid it upon her. And she carried it and went into the city (Ruth 3:15).*

February 21, 2005:

Dearest Sweetest Father:

This has been a long, strange winter. Very sad in many ways. You have spoken of a difference, a withdrawal—a Veil of Eternal Justice has been mentioned. So why do I wonder at the difference, the tone, the atmosphere all around, everywhere. I know this must sound like depression, Father, but it is not. We are like frogs that were put in a pot of cool water and the temperature was slowly raised. But we don't jump out to save ourselves. We can't jump out of...earthly life. But should we be jumping out of this culture, this global culture? Isn't there goodness and sanity anywhere? Can Your Kingdom come in such a world as this? Without forcibly or miraculously changing so many minds and hearts? We are all caught in a web of our own device and making, and it is strangling the very breath out of us.

Father, please don't leave us, please don't withdraw from us. We need You— isn't it us who have withdrawn from You? Aren't we the prodigal children? How, if we choose, can we find You if you have left our family home. I thought You would be waiting with Your arms wide open for us.

You said a veil—perhaps to hide our view of our home and You so we can't come to You or the coming is delayed so that we must feel the consequences of our foolishness longer.

I don't know, Father, I don't question Your Wisdom, but these children of Yours are playing with lethal toys and I don't think many of them have the intention or motivation of surrendering themselves to Your peace and love. Too much will. Too much pride. Too much self-love. A fading memory of You—-

Dearest Father, I love You; I adore You; I worship You!

Remember, the time and the place are no longer chosen by you, as this pains

Me. You are not forgotten—merely used in a wholly different way for new purposes. You will see as the days pass and the nights shorten. Bring me souls, Barbara Rose. Like petals on the flower; bouquets of the Heart. Bring me souls so that they may be transformed in My Love and Mercy. Pray for all those who do not know Me or who have turned away. Pray diligently and without ceasing for the time is near when I will apologize no longer for the behavior and beliefs of my lost ones—they are closest to My Heart—for they love but it is not Love. It is hate turned inward. Now go, sleep, rest your heart and wait in My Peace for times that I have chosen for your work. That which is hidden still remains, though unseen to the human eye.

Shalom.

READING:—*6 And in knowledge, abstinence; and in abstinence, patience; and in patience, godliness (2 Peter 1:6).*

February 25, 2005

Papa:

Life is complicated—all the choices and decisions. I love You, Papa.

Daughter of My Heart:

Do you see me?

No, Father, I see only a fog.

Do you wish to see Me?

Yes, Father.

Then see with the eyes of your soul, child.

I don't think I know how to do that anymore.

When you see, you must allow your soul, which illumines the mind, to capture what is there but unseen by the human eye. I AM here now and always. Try this, little one. Practice with Me now. Close your human eyes and see with the heart—your soul.

March 9, 2005

Last evening after I said my Chaplet, I saw something disturbing. Our Father asked me if I could see Him. Again, I felt great difficulty, fogginess, and a sense of chaos. And I realized that it was on purpose that I was having difficulty—for then I saw people being lifted up, floating away from earth—and I somehow realized these individuals were not good. Then I saw down upon a mass of people, some in business suits, milling around aimlessly, looking for someone or something they couldn't find. There was a sense of hopelessness and apathy—though still some attempt to find someone or something. It appeared to be a city.

Next I saw an ugly grey, but powerful, energized scene of mechanization and things that moved dangerously, robotic, and no feeling of humanity or life.

And then I saw Our Lord Jesus and He seemed to be looking down upon the first scene as on a steel globe, the top piece was missing, like a slice.

I do not fully understand what I saw but my sense was that there was an (1) evil presence on this earth, (2) we were a lost people without a presence of God, and (3) humanity, life, was missing in what I saw—a vast city of machines and robots. It was as if the machines/robots were building more machines/robots that were earth movers or diggers. And I felt deeply our impaired ability to experience God in these times, though we tried. Something we had taken for granted. We have done it to ourselves. This seems to be a great trial for humanity, almost like an exile similar to our first one described in Genesis—when God was so readily available to us and we rejected Him. And God placed us outside the Garden and we wandered... aimlessly for so long. Surviving only. Even though He was always nearby.

I cannot begin to express how painful and devastating this was—something we had taken for granted, especially in the grace-filled years leading up until now. I asked Our Father if it was His Will, if He would spare me any more looks at this tragic event—it was like looking at Purgatory or even Hell. I had never experienced anything like this before.

I pray to You, our Dearest Sweetest Father, to please have mercy on your children—because that is what we are—lacking maturity, judgment, sense. And most of all, whether we realize it or not, we cannot exist without You. Please help us.

Allow us to come back home, imbued and enriched and transformed with your grace and Spirit—please Father.

Or, I wonder—if it is too late for hearts to be converted. No, I do not think so. But it will be very difficult now and without the consolations and confirmation we had previously in the past years. Father, please save us from ourselves. We are Your children. You made us in your likeness and image. Take us by the hand and walk with us through our maturation into adulthood (realization, clarity, conviction). I choose this for all Your children if I am allowed; I say "Yes" for all of us—for we know not what we do—but slowly our eyes are being opened and we feel the loss, we see the loss, we hear the loss. Papa, please bring us home; shepherd us home—even your little lost ones who wander far, far from You. Help us to love You as You love us.

The time is coming when the Church, Your Church, will be fractured—bickering, fighting—-no sense of the Sacred or the Good. As if the Spirit is but a shadow over the Body of Christ. A body defiled, suffering, and almost unconscious.

Oh, Father, what a sad condition for us all. Please help us, despite ourselves. We need You so much. I love You; I adore You; I worship You, Father of Our Lord Jesus Christ—Our Father. Amen.

March 9, 2005 [later]

Dearest Father:

I have had an unbidden enlightenment—powerful. I am still in awe of it. From out of the middle of Salvation History comes an explosion, a flash, an insertion of the Incarnate Word. It is a tremendous flash of light that sends forth and takes in everything. And this sending forth and taking in is an energy, a dynamism, a life force that draws everything in and sends everything out—in, out. Like a two-way black hole—only this one is white, so white. I see how Abraham's sacrifice is positioned in the middle between the Garden exile and the Crucifixion and Resurrection. And the Holocaust of God's children stands in the middle between the Crucifixion and Resurrection and the Coming of the New Jerusalem.

Now I understand—"Time bending back upon itself" in a dynamism of Redemption and Return. What preceded Abraham's sacrifice? That period we are now in—and God saved mankind so man could begin again (Noah).

Oh, but what man was after the Fall—only this time having been redeemed and imbued with grace. But in this time, this counterpart of the Flood, it was evil, not a loving father, that sacrificed the children of God in the Holocaust. It was the anti-offering/sacrifice—redeemed by so many blessed souls, murdered, butchered, burned.

Now I understand the significance of the figure "eight" and time bending back upon itself. Clearly, we are heading for the great "Fiat," despite the godless world we have created and live in and die in.

To re-enter into true intimacy with God, we must offer and keep our Fiat. That is our only hope—it always was.

Humanity has squandered its inheritance....

2006

THE CALL WILL GO OUT

March 6, 2006

I have avoided you, My God, My Father, because in my pain, I believed that my suffering was somehow connected to You. But even this brings me no relief. I am deep, deep into the desert. Please help me. My discomfort is so intense.

Father, please, I beg You, lift this sorrow and loneliness. Let me live again, and smile, and be joyful.

I love you.

Barbara Rose

May 1, 2006

Dearest Sweetest Father:

I love you; I adore you; I worship you.

Please come to my aid and assistance, Father. I am in great need of You.

I wish only to be poor, quiet, and loving.

I just want to be quiet and to be with You again. I miss You.

In trying to be Your hands and feet on earth (in a microscopic, insignificant way), I lost You in the process.

Is this how it should be? Is this a sacrifice I'm called to offer? Or am I ignoring the most important thing—You?

In this, I am puzzled. I just know my mind and body cry out—"No more!"

I feel like I'm in a plague of locusts, chatter that never ceases. No time for recollection and meditation, only react and respond—action.

Father, I don't ask You for the privilege of a miracle—only help in knowing what Your Will is for me.

Wouldn't it be terrible, too terrible, if I end my life and all this energy expended was put in the wrong place? Let me know, Papa. Please.

I look to You for Your mercy and I beg that You not abandon me. Oh, please don't abandon Me, ever, dear Lord.

Your daughter who loves You above all else—Barbara.

I find myself at His feet and His face shines and He says: *Care for those I send you, daughter.*

[I hear "Blessed is He Who Comes in the name of the Lord; Hosanna in the highest."]

Daughter, believe. Lift up your eyes to heaven and there all shall be revealed to you, little one—all that your tiny heart needs to know for now. Eyes on heaven only for a time and the picture will become clearer. Remember, I AM with you though My Presence may seem faint and in the shadows. I AM here and will remain with you all your days and thereafter because you are My daughter in whom I AM well pleased. Be not afraid, My daughter, daughter of My Heart.

You have pleased Me in coming to Me in such tenderness and need. Yes, this pleases Me. I place you nearer My Heart, though it may seem farther.

Your journey is not yet done; there are many fruits yet undeveloped. With time this, too, will be revealed. Say My Name frequently and draw near to My Divine Paternal Heart for sustenance and comfort. Feel it, experience it in your soul—not your body, for that, daughter, will be your cross on earth. Offer all to Me for the salvation of souls and pray, pray, pray that My Will is done on earth as it is in heaven.

My children stray ever further. Soon the call will go out, yet again, and all the world will tremble in its intensity—My Desire. All will experience this wave, this vibration of My Love. Know that I AM here once again in a way that is

Special to complete My plan for My children. They will come home because I WILL it so and will send My angels to gather up all who wander. They will kick and scream, but the intensity of this call will be most convincing—for most, not all. Believe, little one. Come again to My heart and listen for My voice—it beckons you and all.

Remember the placement of this day—between My dearest Catherine of Siena and Joseph, My son. Follow their examples. Intimacy and love of God and your family—always in My Will.

Believe, little daughter of My Heart.

Save the people, all, for My sake and that of the whole world.

Shalom.

READING:—"*O Lord, Father, and sovereign ruler of My Life, leave me not to their counsel; nor suffer me to fall by them who will set scourges over My thoughts, and the disciplines of wisdom over My Heart, that they spare me not in their ignorances and that their sins may not appear...*" (Ecclesiasticus 23).

June 10, 2006 (Pentecost Sunday):

Dearest Sweetest God My Father:

Why have I been away from You so long? I don't know why; I just know I can't change it by will or imagination. It is not in my control. I know You are there, always, but I feel as though I've lost You, like a fading memory or dream. Still real, yet faint, behind a veil I can no longer see or hear through. Perhaps this is the way of all Your children while on earth. Perhaps what I experienced years ago was an anomaly, an aberration. I don't think anything else I write will be published or made known in my lifetime, if ever. I no longer have Your Grace in this regard. My only hope is that when I die someday, I will once again know You as I once did.

As always I am a weak, timid mouse, cringing away from the crushing responsibilities of my life.... I have ended up where I began so long ago. The circle of my outside interactions is narrowing once more.....

I've asked my dearest Mother Mary to please intercede for me. Always I am complaining and asking for help, never thanking You for what I have. I'm sorry, Father. Please forgive me. And on this Feast of Pentecost, please send Your Holy Spirit into my heart, soul, mind, and body. I ask this in Jesus' name, so that I may know, love, and honor You more and more every single day of my existence. I need You so much, Father. I am nothing without You—an empty, vacant shell, a shadow. Oh, please, Father, fill me with your Divine Light and Love so that Your Presence may live in me, love in me. Now and forever. Amen.

Let this be a lesson to you, little daughter of My Heart. Remember to countenance all that is brought before you. For it is I that place it there. When you tremble in fear and confusion it is because you have lost Me, My hand, My Heart—in your eagerness to please and accomplish. Only I can bring joy and happiness to your life—for Mine is the Kingdom, the Power, and the Glory— now and forever.

READING:—*60 And I will remember my covenant with thee in the days of thy youth: and I will establish with thee an everlasting covenant. 61 And thou shalt remember thy ways, and be ashamed: when thou shalt receive thy sisters, thy elder and thy younger: and I will give them to thee for daughters, but not by thy covenant. 62 And I will establish my covenant with thee: and thou shalt know that I am the Lord, 63 That thou mayest remember, and be confounded, and mayest no more open thy mouth because of thy confusion, when I shall be pacified toward thee for all that thou hast done, saith the Lord God." Ezekial 16: 56-63*

July 29, 2006

Dearest Sweetest God My Father:

Some of my blood test results came back as abnormal. This accounts for the fatigue and aches I experience. But what do I do with this information? I don't know. I should be happy that I have had a good, long life. The question now, it seems, is what I do with the rest of my life.

First, I hope to avoid being a burden on anyone. Second, I hope to enrich my spiritual life and find peace. Third, I wish will all My heart to have a good, happy family, where there is faith, hope, joy, love, and peace.

I love you, Father—

October 7, 2006

Dearest God My Father:

I break my silence. I am so unworthy. I pity myself. I dwell on my illness. I feel as though my life has been ruined—I'm dying. I feel as though I am dying—and worst of all my soul has been so very dry. For so long. I need You—but then again, it is what I want, want, want.

I am a miserable human being—

I don't feel anything at all. Only terrible, overhwelming, frightening fatigue.

I am here and if You wish to speak to me, I will try and listen. I am so sorry. Help me, please, Father.

Daughter—what are you sorry for?

Not feeling anything.

Why should you sorrow over that?

Because it's as if I don't care.
But I know you care.
Even now my hand can barely write. It's as if my will is gone.

Remove all obstacles. Trust in Me.

What obstacles, Father?

The ones that cloud your mind.

What are those?

Your fear of death.

But I don't think I'm afraid of death. I just want to sleep.

You are running away, child.

Maybe I am afraid and don't know it.

You please Me, Barbara Rose.

Why, Father?

Because you look at life as if it were a staged play with certain episodes to unfold according to a pre-ordained plot. Life is not a play with a plot. It is experience, every moment, lived in grace and My Will. If you detach your spirit from Me, I cannot touch you, embrace you, tell you that you are my precious daughter.

Try, try very hard to reach Me in your heart. You may do this by praying more frequently and going to the Sacrament of Reconciliation tomorrow. This will please Me because you are moving toward My healing love. Make the effort and I will meet you more than half way—

I will come and comfort you daily and in your hour of need. For your time is apppointed by Me—and only Me—and you know not when that is. Live as I have instructed you in faith and belief of a better life in the next world. This is but a shadow of what is to come.

Dream now and I will awaken you with a sign for you to hold tight to in the days and weeks ahead. Yours daughter is not an easy road, but you knew that. This is no surprise. And with this knowledge you will grow in deeper love and compassion for all those who suffer. You have tried to run away. I understand. But I call you to this life of suffering and denial for a purpose greater than you realize.

The greatness is not in you, Barbara Rose. It is in the intention to love and be loved by Me, despite the cost. Will you say "yes" again? I give you this choice.

I'm afraid, Father. I am afraid.

Fix your eyes on heaven, child, and be not afraid.

[I hear "misericordia."]

READING:—*"1 Now the publicans and sinners drew near unto him to hear him. 2 And the Pharisees and the scribes murmured, saying: This man receiveth sinners, and eateth with them. 3 And he spoke to them this parable, saying: 4 What man of you that hath an hundred sheep: and if he shall lose one of them, doth he not leave the ninety-nine in the desert, and go after that which was lost, until he find it? 5 And when he hath found it, lay it upon his shoulders, rejoicing:*

6 And coming home, call together his friends and neighbours, saying to them: Rejoice with me, because I have found my sheep that was lost? 7 I say to you, that even so there shall be joy in heaven upon one sinner that doth penance, more than upon ninety-nine just who need not penance. 8 Or what woman having ten groats; if she lose one groat, doth not light a candle, and sweep the house, and seek diligently until she find it? 9 And when she hath found it, call together her friends and neighbours, saying: Rejoice with me, because I have found the groat which

I had lost. 10 So I say to you, there shall be joy before the angels of God upon one sinner doing penance. 11 And he said: A certain man had two sons: 12 And the younger of them said to his father: Father, give me the portion of substance that falleth to me. And he divided unto them his substance. 13 And not many days after, the younger son, gathering all together, went abroad into a far country: and there wasted his substance, living riotously. 14 And after he had spent all, there came a mighty famine in that country; and he began to be in want. 15 And he went and cleaved to one of the citizens of that country. And he sent him into his farm to feed swine.

16 And he would fain have filled his belly with the husks the swine did eat; and no man gave unto him. 17 And returning to himself, he said: How many hired servants in my father's house abound with bread, and I here perish with hunger? 18 I will arise, and will go to my father, and say to him: Father, I have sinned against heaven, and before thee: 19 I am not worthy to be called thy son: make me as one of thy hired servants. 20 And rising up he came to his father. And when he was yet a great way off, his father saw him, and was moved with compassion, and running to him fell upon his neck, and kissed him.

21 And the son said to him: Father, I have sinned against heaven, and before thee, I am not now worthy to be called thy son. 22 And the father said to his servants: Bring forth quickly the first robe, and put it on him, and put a ring on his hand, and shoes on his feet: 23 And bring hither the fatted calf, and kill it, and let us eat and make merry: 24 Because this my son was dead, and is come to life again: was lost, and is found. And they began to be merry. 25 Now his elder son was in the field, and when he came and drew nigh to the house, he heard music and dancing:

26 And he called one of the servants, and asked what these things meant. 27 And he said to him: Thy brother is come, and thy father hath killed the fatted calf, because he hath received him safe. 28 And he was angry, and would not go in. His father therefore coming out began to entreat him. 29 And he answering, said to his father: Behold, for so many years do I serve thee, and I have never transgressed thy commandment, and yet thou hast never given me a kid to make merry with my friends: 30 But as soon as this thy son is come, who hath devoured his substance with harlots, thou hast killed for him the fatted calf.

31 But he said to him: Son, thou art always with me, and all I have is thine. 32 But it was fit that we should make merry and be glad, for this thy brother was dead and is come to life again; he was lost, and is found" (Luke 15).

YES!

October 7, 2006

Dearest Sweetest Father:

I love You; I adore You; I worship You. I see your hand this morning regarding.....Thank you so much. I enjoyed our conversation last night and slept very well for the first time....

Father, please forgive me, but I feel so weak and tired today. Would you please hear my confession?

Yes. Barbara, there is wickedness and there is light and good. You know the difference between the two. Run from the dark into the light. Stay close to My Divine Paternal Heart, and I will bless you, little one.

I have remained with you even in your darkest moments. Believe in me; experience My Love for you and grant it freely to all those who are in your life—past, present, and future.

Now recite the prayer closest to My Heart; the one given you by My Beloved Son Jesus and He will pray with you.

Blessed are you, daughter of My Heart. Now be at peace and know I AM with you all the days, ever.

[Father, I love you.]

I know that, little one. Now rest in My Divine Peace and Sustenance. Rest and believe.

[Last night I dreamed of a birth. My child, my daughter, was giving birth but she was being attacked and beaten up while she delivered. In the dream I felt outraged that anyone would hurt my child, especially in such a vulnerable situation. [How much more must Our Father feel for us?] That's all I remember.

October 8, 2006

Dearest Sweetest Father:

You elude me, though I know You are near. I wish to be closer, Lord. Please draw me closer and show me the way. What would you like me to do, Father? What is Your Will for me regarding my job and family? I wish I didn't have to make these choices. I think I choose by not choosing —but my energy continues to flag and I worry I won't be able to do any of it. Please guide me.

Kiss them all for me.

Who, Father?

The little ones, the weak.

READING:—"*1 Now it is found in the descriptions of Jeremias the prophet, that he commanded them that went into captivity, to take the fire, as it hath been signified, and how he gave charge to them that were carried away into captivity. 2 And how he gave them the law that they should not forget the commandments of the Lord, and that they should not err in their minds, seeing the idols of gold, and silver, and the ornaments of them. 3 And with other such like speeches, he exhorted them that they would not remove the law from their heart. 4 It was also contained in the same writing, how the prophet, being warned by God, commanded that the tabernacle and the ark should accompany him, till he came forth to the mountain where Moses went up, and saw the inheritance of God. 5 And when Jeremias came thither he found a hollow cave: and he carried in thither the tabernacle, and the ark, and the altar of incense, and so stopped the door.*

6 Then some of them that followed him, came up to mark the place: but they could not find it. 7 And when Jeremias perceived it, he blamed them, saying: The place shall be unknown, till God gather together the congregation of the people, and receive them to mercy. 8 And then the Lord will shew these things, and the majesty of the Lord shall appear, and there shall be a cloud as it was also shewed to Moses, and he shewed it when Solomon prayed that the place might be sanctified to the great God. 9 For he treated wisdom in a magnificent manner: and like a wise man, he offered the sacrifice of the dedication, and of the finishing of the temple. 10 And as Moses prayed to the Lord and fire came down from heaven, and consumed the holocaust: so Solomon also prayed, and fire came down from heaven and consumed the holocaust.

11 And Moses said: Because the sin offering was not eaten, it was consumed. 12 So Solomon also celebrated the dedication eight days. 13 And these same things were set down in the memoirs and commentaries of Nehemias: and how he made a library, and gathered together out of the countries, the books both of the prophets, and of David, and the epistles of the kings. and concerning the holy gifts. 14 And in like manner Judas also gathered together all such things as were lost by the war we had, and they are in our possession. 15 Wherefore if you want these things, send some that may fetch them to you.

16 As we are then about to celebrate the purification, we have written unto you: and you shall do well, if you keep the same days. 17 And we hope that God who hath delivered his people, and hath rendered to all the inheritance, and the kingdom, and the priesthood, and the sanctuary, 18 As he promised in the law, will shortly have mercy upon us, and will gather us together from every land under heaven into the holy place. 19 For he hath delivered us out of great perils, and hath cleansed the place. 20 Now as concerning Judas Machabeus. and his brethren, and the purification of the great temple, and the dedication of the altar:" (2 Mac 14).

November 11, 2006

Dearest Sweetest Father:

Today during and after Communion, I had an experience. Again, I saw the little cottage. I enter through a hedgerow covered with flowers, small and delicate, of every color. Especially pinks and purples. But the scent is what always makes me smile. I can see into the small backyard, which is fenced around in what appears to be like a square by the hedgerow. There is a birdfeeder—black wrought iron. And then behind me, entering the hedgerow entrance, I sense someone. I see a large man, fair, and strong. And then I begin to spread what seems like the wings of a bird and begin to rise up and then everything changes and I am descending into a dark, old, stone, narrow stairway and it is a burial chamber with a small window. There is a slab and I am laid out on it, my feet facing the small glassless window in the right wall. I have on a long dress and on my chest are long green reeds. And going in I was terrified. The large man I believe now is Gabriel—he touches my hand to comfort me. I realize I do not have to do this—but God says I will stay here for three days but on the third day I will rise. Three days in death. And I am given a choice. I am very frightened and I don't know what this means—literally? I don't know but I say yes and then I realize the reeds are from my previous visions of the wetland area that always precede my meeting with God (David running ahead of me, the Church at the top of the hill, and after the desert with Our Lady before the ocean shore). The reeds are evidence of water.

Father, I don't understand what this imagery means for me. I love You.

READING:—*"29 And I will hide my face no more from them, for I have poured out my spirit upon all the house of Israel, saith the Lord God. (Ezechial 39:29).*

November 8, 2006

Dearest Father:

You told me to just let go and let the images go—I will try. I see now that I have been strongly resisting them for some time. But why?

I am fatigued almost all the time now. I don't know how much longer I can go on feeling so tired.

I Am Reality

January 26, 2007

Dearest Sweetest Father:

I have taken a medical leave from work and family responsibilities. I have been exhausted—physically, mentally, emotionally, and spiritually for a very long time now. Whatever resources I had are gone, greatly depleted—barely existing.

I am done.

What does this mean—I am done? I don't think even I know—only that I can no longer do what I have been doing. Period.

This wasn't a frivolous choice. I hit the wall. Any thought of returning to the life I had and my mind shuts down—won't allow it. I cannot push myself any more. I could not keep up.

I am in a healing phase now. How would I describe this? The only thing I can compare it to is an animal who has been injured and is curled up in a ball and can't move, just keeps licking its wound. And at the same time is curled up to protect itself from further onslaught. So I guess I'm (1) trying to rest and do what I need to do to heal my wounded body, mind, and soul, and (2) protect myself from further injury.

I also have no idea who I am anymore. Is this fragmentation? Perhaps, but I think I had to break apart so the pieces could be put back together in a different way.

An insight I've had is that I don't seem to care about things I thought were important before. What I mean is that I let go of responsibilities that were crushing me to death.

Where are the pieces going to fall? I don't know yet. I can't see an outline or pattern. I could use some fatherly advice if you are willing to share it.

[I am in a sunny open field bordered by trees, tallish field grass and "some" flowers and I am lying down in the grass—but my mind keeps chattering away and I still can't find God. And then I sense Him and He says that first, I must find myself and then I will find Him.]

But who am I, Father? I can't find my outline or borders—I am a shadow person, pale and translucent. Who am I? Is it too late in my life to find out? I have always been defined by circumstances—but who am I? Help me, God, please. Help me find myself so I can find You.

READING:—*21 How is the faithful city, that was full of judgment, become a harlot? justice dwelt in it, but now murderers. 22 Thy silver is turned into dress: thy wine is mingled with water. 23 Thy princes are faithless, companions of thieves: they all love bribes, the run after rewards. They judge not for the fatherless: and the widow's cometh not in to them. 24 Therefore saith the Lord the God of hosts, the mighty one of Israel: Ah! I will comfort myself over my adversaries: and I will be revenged of my enemies. 25 And I will turn my hand to thee, and I will purge away thy dress, and I will take away all thy tin.*

26 And I will restore thy judges as they were before, and thy counselors as of old. After this thou shalt be called the city of the just, a faithful city. 27 Sion shall be redeemed in judgment, and they shall bring her back in justice. 28 And he shall destroy the wicked, and the sinners together: and they that have forsaken the Lord, shall be consumed. 29 For they shall be confounded for the idols, to which they have sacrificed: and you shall be ashamed of the gardens which you have chosen. 30 When you shall be as an oak with the leaves falling off, and as a garden without water. " (Is 1:21-30).

Follow Me.

But how?

Be.

What, Father?

My child, that is who you really are—a child of God. Discover what this means and you will have all the answers you desire.

Shalom, little daughter of My Heart.

January 31, 2007

Dearest Sweetest Papa:

Oh, I am so scared...my poor son....

Peace is upon you in gentle ways, lacking only in your openness to see through the darkness that has descended all around you. True, I have allowed this for a purpose. So that you would come to believe that endurance must be tried and tested to endure. You have been protected for a time, child, from the onslaughts of the Evil One, but I have allowed these trials so that you see with the eyes of your soul once again. What do you see?

[I see a blanket, a murkiness, a heaviness all around me and my family.] I'm scared, Papa.

This is why I say this to you, child of My Heart—believe and bring yourself ever closer to My Divine Paternal Heart. The time is coming when you will be tested in a way that is beyond your prior experience. But you have done well.

How?

By believing when there was no "feeling" of belief. Of knowing when nothing made sense. Despite the graces to assist you, you chose to believe and persevere. This trial is now over and new ones begin. But have not all your trials ended in the goodness of My Heart, Barbara Rose?

Father, I feel like a virtual wreck. Please, I am not up to any more tests or trials—I am weak.

You have Me, your Father, Who loves you and Who is proud of you.

Hold tight the reigns I have given you. They will bring you to Me if you use a gentle hand and guide your soul along the path to My Divine Paternal Heart. Have I answered your question?

Father, I still don't know what to do in a practical sense.

Sleep, child, and all will be made clear to you. This, I promise, Not one drop of your love will be wasted. This I promise. Now sleep.

Good night, Father. Please be close to me, especially tonight. Let me feel

Your Presence. My heart is breaking for my son. Please help and comfort him, Father. Please. Please. My mother's heart is breaking.

READING:—*"2 Be instant in prayer; watching in it with thanksgiving"* (Colossians 4:2).

April 8, 2007 (Easter and my son's birthday)

This weekend I ran into a literal wall, Father. I cracked my head and cheek hard, very hard. I never saw the wall. Never. What a shock that was, like running into an invisible window. Regardless, I ended up in the Emergency Room at the hospital. I had been running into the garage to get into my daughter's car so we could go and buy yarn for a blanket I was crocheting my granddaughter. I knew the second my head hit the corner of the cabinet in the garage—I ran full speed into it—that it was a "wake-up" call. I had to stop running around like a chicken with my head cut off, frantically.

I was very, very frightened that I had really hurt myself—my forehead ballooned out and my vision was obscured by an egg-like protrusion. It felt like I cracked my skull and cheekbone. I was certain I was bleeding inside my head.

I couldn't believe I had done this to myself—could inflict this much damage on myself. At the Emergency Room I kept saying I was sorry.

Father, if you would like to speak to me, I am listening.

Little one, I AM here.

Where, Father?

Beside you, in you. Why do you seem surprised? Has it not always been so? You dream of dreams and not of Me Who am. I AM reality. Take time to look for me. I AM everywhere, in everything, in all times. What does this mean to you, in your life? Your aspirations? Your sorrows? I AM in all these experiences.

....

Beyond the darkness, there is light. I AM the Light. I am with your always. You are not an orphan, little daughter of My Heart.

When life presses in on you, you must push back, gently, yet forcefully to maintain your sacred space with Me. This life that oppresses you can be embraced as if a dance. There is a rhythm unfolding. Listen for this music and participate in the dance of life.

When I call you, you will have no doubt that a new task is asked of you. A greater one than before—different in scope. You will know, child, because it could not have emerged of your own imaginings.

You feel as if you are drowning in suffering?

Yes.

Be patient, trust, and I promise that I will lead you to the peace you desire. Be prepared and wait on your Lord. Remember, you will know because it is beyond your means to contrive.

Be inspired. I AM with you and I bless you with My Fatherly blessing.

READING: —*"1 A prayer of Jesus the son of Sirach. I will give glory to thee, O Lord, O King, and I will praise thee, O God my Saviour. 2 I will give glory to thy name: for thou hast been a helper and protector to me. 3 And hast preserved my body from destruction, from the snare of an unjust tongue, and from the lips of them that forge lies, and in the sight of them that stood by, thou hast been my helper. 4 And thou hast delivered me, according to the multitude of the mercy of thy name, from them that did roar, prepared to devour. 5 Out of the hands of them that sought my life, and from the gates of afflictions, which compassed me about:*

6 From the oppression of the flame which surrounded me, and in the midst of the fire I was not burnt. 7 From the depth of the belly of hell, and from an unclean tongue, and from lying words, from an unjust king, and from a slanderous tongue: 8 My soul shall praise the Lord even to death. 9 And my life was drawing near to hell beneath. 10 They compassed me on every side, and there was no one that would help me. I looked for the succour of men, and there was none.

11 I remembered thy mercy, O Lord, and thy works, which are from the beginning of the world. 12 How thou deliverest them that wait for thee, O Lord, and savest them out of the hands of the nations. 13 Thou hast exalted my dwelling place upon the earth and I have prayed for death to pass away. 14 I called upon the Lord, the father of my Lord, that he would not leave me in the day of my trouble, and in the time of the proud without help. 15 I will praise thy name continually, and will praise it with thanksgiving, and my prayer was heard.

16 And thou hast saved me from destruction, and hast delivered me from the evil time. 17 Therefore I will give thanks, and praise thee, and bless the name of the

Lord. 18 When I was yet young, before I wandered about, I sought for wisdom openly in my prayer. 19 I prayed for her before the temple, and unto the very end I will seek after her, and she flourished as a grape soon ripe. 20 My heart delighted in her, my foot walked in the right way, from my youth up I sought after her.

21 I bowed down my ear a little, and received her. 22 I found much wisdom in myself, and I profited much therein. 23 To him that giveth me wisdom, will I give glory. 24 For I have determined to follow her: I have had a zeal for good, and shall not be confounded. 25 My soul hath wrestled for her, and in doing it I have been confirmed.

26 I stretched forth my hands on high, and I bewailed my ignorance of her. 27 I directed my soul to her, and in knowledge I found her. 28 I possessed my heart with her from the beginning: therefore I shall not be forsaken. 29 My entrails were troubled in seeking her: therefore shall I possess a good possession. 30 The Lord hath given me a tongue for my reward: and with it I will praise him.

31 Draw near to me, ye unlearned, and gather yourselves together into the house of discipline. 32 Why are ye slow? and what do you say of these things? your souls are exceeding thirsty. 33 I have opened my mouth, and have spoken: buy her for yourselves without silver, 34 And submit your neck to the yoke, and let your soul receive discipline: for she is near at hand to be found. 35 Behold with your eyes how I have laboured a little, and have found much rest to myself.

36 Receive ye discipline as a great sum of money, and possess abundance of gold by her. 37 Let your soul rejoice in his mercy, and you shall not be confounded in his praise. 38 Work your work before the time, and he will give you your reward in his time" (Ecclesiasticus 51).

April 21, 2007

Dearest Sweetest Papa:

During prayer, I experienced a "briar patch." You were with me and I chose to enter the briar patch. I swatted the branches and thorns aside, but only with my hands, arms, and head. I had nothing else. And as I progressed, the foliage became thicker and thicker—almost causing me to fight my way through horizontally—my body squeezing through, as if crawling. My feet no longer on the ground.

And I turned around, almost in exasperation, to ask why You were not leading or helping me. But the reply was that it was my choice and that you would be with me and follow me through this morass—but it was not to be that You would be the pathfinder. Somehow I felt this wasn't fair.

Then I realized that I didn't know where I was going and had no point of reference. So even if I could see or hear, I wouldn't know where to go. No God; no compass. Lost. But I had to keep moving because if I didn't, the thorns would pierce my body deeply. If I kept moving, they merely scratched me and lifted me up above the ground. To stop would mean to fall down into the quagmire, my sheer weight bearing me down, the thorns pressing into me, impressing me.

But how, Father, can I keep going if I have nowhere to go? Where am I leading us? This is senseless, meaningless, futile.

Oh, Daughter of My Heart, move closer to Me.

How? If I slow down I'll be lost.

Will I not catch you and lift you up?

But I thought this was all my choice, and I don't even know what my choice is or why I made it.

Slow. Slow a bit, child. Feel my hand upon you. Do you fall?

No, Father. I'm suspended and feel no pain.

Now turn around and see my eyes. Are they not comfort? Are they not Love? Are they not strength?

Yes, Papa.

Drop.

Drop what, Father?

Drop the stone that is in your heart. Give it to Me to hold for you.

What stone? And if I had a stone, wouldn't I fall faster?

But it is the stone that makes you frantically rush forward. Do you see?

But why did I enter the brambled forest?

What were you looking for, child?

I don't know. I think maybe it was a shortcut.

To where?

I don't know.

Perhaps you should stop now and think.

About what, Father?

What you are doing.

But I don't know. I have no idea. My head spins with everything I'm involved with—all the things that I'm doing.

Peace, Daughter of My Heart. My Peace I give you. Can you feel it?

Oh, yes, Father. No pain, just peace. Father, how do I discover where and what I should be doing? So far I haven't done a very good job.

Blink.

Blink, Father?

During your lives, you have moments of sight and blindness. This is necessary to ensure clear vision and rest. Is this not true?

Yes, Father.

Now, your eyes have been closed in reaction to an injury to your sight. Your eyes water, they tear, they blink. But then...they open and see again.

Father, what injured my sight?

The ability to see is a gift, freely given by me. This gift if not used, if discarded, may be retrieved by the giver—if it has been cast off.

Did I do that, Father?

Yes, daughter.

How? Why?

You ran without looking into the wall, did you not?

Yes, Father.

You ran into the briar patch, did you not?

Yes, Father. I did.

STOP RUNNING, DAUGHTER!

Walk with Me. See the brambles fall away, revealing a path beneath.

Yes, Father. Where does this path lead?

It is a path made by Me—well worn. It will take you home, if you choose to follow it. Do you have sight once more?

I don't know, but I see the path and I feel You, sense You, behind me.

Along this path there will be pauses, time to pray and reflect. This is the path. Without it, the path will be no more. Wisdom is knowing that what awaits you is greater than the path that takes you there.

What does that mean, Father?

The path is not an end, but a means. There is a purpose for your movement, your choices. This will give you comfort and encouragement. And I AM the Omega—I AM behind you and before you. If you remain on the path and pause when prompted or inspired, you cannot be lost again.

I was lost, wasn't I, Father?

For a long time, little one. Yes. Take Me back into your heart and rest in Mine.

Father, please promise me that these times of prayer and reflection will be clear. Please—I am frightened that I will miss them and be lost again.

Daughter, child, Discipline. Rhythm, Heartbeat. Life. Keep My Precious Blood flowing through your heart by contractions of your heart, giving birth to much love of Me and My children.

Now, daughter of My Divine Paternal Heart, let me finish by directing you to a special reading. You will find it in David's Psalm (115/114) in your Bible. This is close to My own thoughts and actions and love for you, as I know and trust you love Me.

Yes, Father, yes.

Shalom. Be at peace, Barbara Rose.

Thank You. Thank You so much, Father.

Be at peace, child. Be at peace in My Divine Paternal Heart.

READING:—*I have loved, because the Lord will hear the voice of my prayer. Because he hath inclined his ear unto me: and in my days I will call upon him. The sorrows of death have compassed me; and the perils of hell have found me. I met with trouble and sorrow: and I called upon the name of the Lord. Oh Lord, deliver my soul. The lord is merciful and just, and our God sheweth mercy. The Lord is the keeper of Little Ones: I was humbled, and he delivered me. Turn oh my soul, into thy rest: for the Lord hath been bountiful to thee. For he hath delivered my soul from death; my eyes from tears, my feet from falling. I will please the Lord in the Land of the Living....You have broken my bonds. I will sacrifice to thee the sacrifices of praise and I will call upon the name of the Lord. I will pay my vows to the Lord in the sight of all his people: in the courts of the house of the Lord, in the midst of thee, O Jerusalem.*